THE NEW INSTITUTION   **Edited by Bernd Scherer, with contributions by Gigi Argyropoulou, Maria Hlavajova, Olaf Nicolai, Adania Shibli, and Eyal Weizman**

The New Institution

**Edited by
Bernd Scherer**

Contents

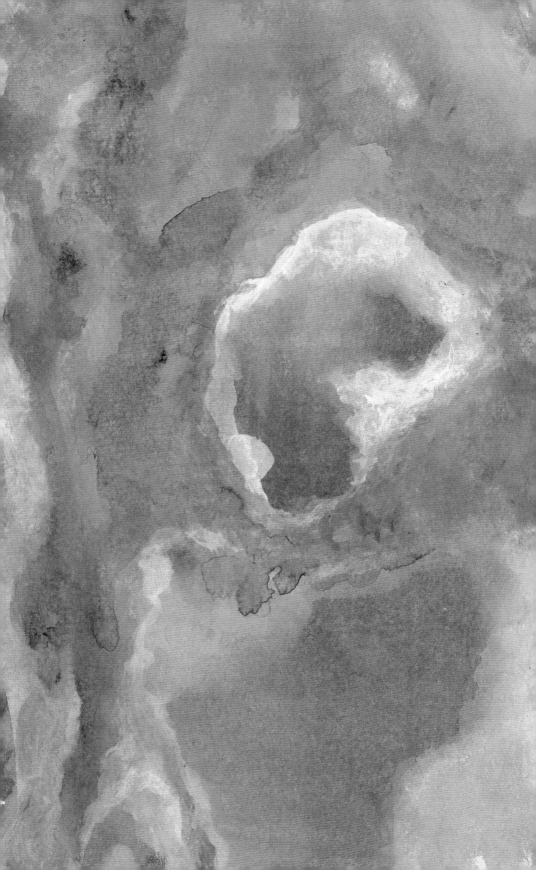

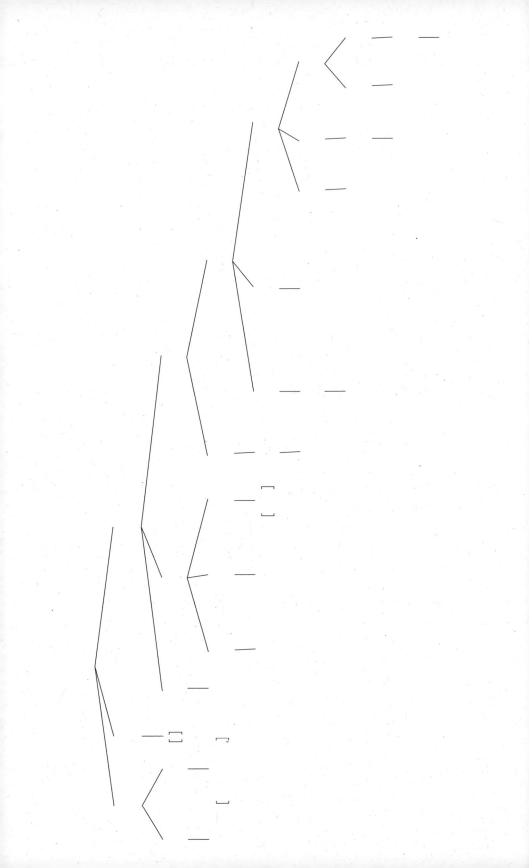

The End of the Monologue:
On the Madness of Normality

The final volume of the DNA series asks: what cultural institutions do we need in order to tackle the crises shaking our societies? Over the past ten years, we at Haus der Kulturen der Welt (HKW) have constantly grappled with this fundamental question and have attempted, both in our work and in conversations with colleagues, to develop practices and forms of presentation that make the problematic situation of institutional work in our time socially negotiable.

Argentine artist Leon Ferrari speaks of the daily madness necessary for everything to seem normal. In this sense, our work at HKW can be understood as an attempt to create cracks in the constructs of normality and thus make the madness at work recognizable. I would like to elaborate on this recent approach with a discussion of two works whose critical gaze on our institution was instrumental in shifting our understanding of the work we do.

In 2015, we invited artist Maria Eichhorn—who designed the German contribution at the Venice Biennale 2022—to create a project about the site on which HKW now stands. Archival research led to the discovery that the former Kongresshalle (Congress Hall), now HKW, was built on the ruins of a Jewish residential quarter that also housed the clinic of sexologist and pioneer of the gay liberation movement, Magnus Hirschfeld.

Whilst Hirschfeld was forced to flee in the 1930s, the Jewish owner of the other buildings was forced to sell her property below market value to a German lawyer. He, in turn, sold the property to the state after the war for a much higher price. The Jewish owner was deported to a concentration camp, and the restitution claim by her sons, who had fled to Latin America, was rejected.

In her work, Maria Eichhorn used markings to make visible the old residential buildings once located on the HKW site. In this way, the violence hidden beneath and within the structures of the building's architecture becomes discernible—a violence of extermination in the name of nationalist ideas.

Eichhorn's project also illustrates the persistence of National Socialism in Germany after 1945. Unlawfully enriched from the proceeds of the property of the Jewish family he had displaced, the German lawyer maintained a renowned law firm in Düsseldorf until the

1970s. Meanwhile, in 1957, the Congress Hall was built as a gift from the United States to the city of Berlin. Eleanor Dulles, a major driving force behind the construction, saw the open-form architecture as a symbol of democratic freedom that would radiate into the Eastern Bloc from its position on the border with East Berlin. Thus, erected on the ruins of a Jewish quarter, the building was intended to mask its past by embodying universalist values in the context of the Cold War. The postwar period was typified by such strategies of forgetting. In the new Federal Republic, they created a surface under which nationalist ideas and National Socialist careers remained hidden for a long time.

In retrospect, it could hardly come as a surprise to attentive observers of German history that a "new" nationalist right wing entered the public stage in the 2010s, seamlessly echoing Nazi ideas and eventually even entering the German Bundestag in the form of the AfD. As a place inscribed with the wounds of this history, HKW therefore gave itself the important task of combating forms of antisemitism and exposing their logics, as was most recently done in the conference "Hijacking Memory."

But there is also a second line of memory inscribed in the Haus. It was referred to in a project by the recently deceased artist Jimmie Durham, an important Indigenous North American artist who had lived in Berlin since the mid-1990s.

In *Building a Nation*, Jimmie Durham problematizes the idea of architecture as an instrument of nation-building, commenting on the Congress Hall and its supposed architectural contribution to the democratization of postwar Germany. The installation consists of civilization's scraps, from wooden panels to broken whiskey bottles to demolished car parts. The assemblage marks the dissolution of Western civilization at its edges, the implosion of the universalist settlers' dream of world domination and colonization.

Durham's work includes a direct reference to an inscription in the building that represents the violence of this universalism. It is a quote from Benjamin Franklin, promoting freedom and calling for a world in which a philosopher may set foot anywhere and say: "This is my country." The installation counters Franklin's statement with quotes in which he and other US leaders describe Native Americans as "savages," even "scum of the earth." He thereby demonstrates the violence that emanates from the Western project of civilization, its exclusion of those deemed outside that civilization and therefore marked for colonization and exploitation.

These two projects illustrate the two aspects inscribed in the demand "Never again," both of which the work of HKW seeks to internalize as part of its driving mission. In addition to the particular understanding that there must never be another Jewish Holocaust, there is also the universalist interpretation: that is, the need to struggle against all forms of genocide, against all the "barbarous acts" of humankind, as stated in the Preamble to the Universal Declaration of Human Rights that was created after the Second World War. Jimmie Durham's work draws attention to the fact that various forms of genocide were part of the Western modernist project from the beginning, a project that excluded large parts of the world from its universalism through racialized colonialism and imperialism.

In May 2022, the project *Die Zivilisationsfrage* dealt with these mechanisms of exclusion that intend to normalize the operational modes of the project of modernity in the sense of Leon Ferrari. At the center of the project was an examination of the recently published book by David Graeber and David Wengrow, *The Dawn of Everything: A New History of Humanity*. Here, the two authors show how, in the context of the European Enlightenment, a standard model of human history was developed that played a fundamental and legitimizing role for such exclusionary processes. Neutralizing criticism from other parts of the world about the lack of freedom and the dominance of private property in Europe, this standard model of the history of civilization uses evolutionist logic to describe a linear development of humanity from simple and primitive to increasingly complex social forms, from egalitarian hunter-gatherer societies to pastoralism and agrarianism to capitalism. In such a narrative, Indigenous societies are assigned to a pre-civilizational state of nature. The continuation of this model was seen in the nineteenth century's "scientific" theories of racism, whose patterns of thought still shape discourses today.

With its narrative, Europe created a world model that both legitimized its colonial and imperial aspirations, and, in the name of a progress it saw itself as spearheading, made any alternative to its position invisible. In this way, the substantial spaces of freedom called for by Indigenous critique were eliminated, and the critical self-reflection of one's own project through exchange with others—genuine enlightenment—was disavowed in the interests of colonial power.

Now at the beginning of the twenty-first century, this has created a dual problem that HKW has dealt with in further projects. On the one hand, the human-made climate crisis and the further effects of unbridled growth show that the one-dimensional Western evolutionist model of civilization is leading us to the brink of collapse, as explored by HKW in the *Anthropocene Project*. At the same time, ever more voices are coming forward from colonized countries that have long been oppressed and exploited, bringing new perspectives into the global discourse that are unwilling to fit into a master narrative in which they are seen as needing to catch up with a West that is always a few steps ahead of them. Thus, a critical examination of the violence and oppression of the past has become necessary for a viable future, as has the design of alternative models of living and thinking.

It is equally in the interests of Western societies and those of formerly exploited and colonized countries that the Western claim to sole representation of reason and symbolic supremacy is left behind. This is a painful process, since old certainties are called into question, existing patterns of orientation lose their relevance, and interpretive authority over discourses must be relinquished.

In this sense, HKW has tasked itself in recent years with questioning the exclusion mechanisms of Western modernity and opening up a new political horizon. The aim is to transform Germany, a country of immigration, from a country that retains a nationally shaped understanding of its own identity into a plural and polyphonic society. However, this project can only succeed if the voices of those who have been colonized, oppressed, and exploited over centuries are included from the very beginning. The digital *Archive of Refuge* project set a very important example in this regard.

The recent work of HKW, briefly outlined here, has aimed to bring home the message that Western-influenced reference systems in art and science, in economics and politics, have put the planet in the crisis it is in today—from climate change to species extinction and unprecedented migration. The exclusion of non-Western societies has played a fundamental role in this. A new concept of dialogue is therefore urgently needed. The previous demand for a "dialogue on an equal footing" with non-Western societies was intended to conceal the fact that it was the West that determined the footing to which the others were to be lifted. Such paternalistic gestures, which appealed to the good and the true in the sense of a false understanding of universalism, are obsolete; they were monologues by the West with itself. We need forms of conversation that reflect the contexts of violence out of which our societies have emerged and that promote a negotiation of new world concepts while recognizing distinct conflicting interests and forms of perception.

In view of our planetary challenges, we must now bring all the voices that are important for the future of our societies to the same table whilst differentiating distinct positions in order to avoid a destructive battle of cultures. This is the only way we can keep spaces for discourse open. This is the only way to develop possible solutions to existential global problems. And only in this way can a piece of meaningful, shared reality be wrested from the madness that we regard as normality.

Due to the cultural but also social and economic disparities of the contexts from which the respective actors come, dialogues that move only on a theoretical, abstract level fall short. Instead, such dialogues must be embedded in practices of shared living and working. Therefore, the logic of short-term projects, in which curators intervene in an existing situation for a few months, also falls short. It is far more important to develop long-term joint working relationships in which a bit of shared reality is produced from a multiplicity of perspectives. We need new forms of working and living communities. The development of a critical public sphere and a shared reality are two sides of the same coin.

The contributions in this volume are about opening and regauging the public sphere to enable polyphonic dialogues and thus diverse perspectives that undermine, counteract, and ideally replace existing structures of power and exclusion. Based on their experiences, the contributors reflect on para-institutional practices in which inclusive forms of social participation can be realized. These are practices of a counter-public that position themselves against a traditional institutional structure perceived as exclusionary and dysfunctional and that seeks to maintain the status quo. The practices are para-institutional because they are not institutionally fixed but are continually developed anew in acts of de- and re-instituting. With diverse voices and dynamic conceptions of reality, frames of reference for respective thoughts and actions must always be renegotiated.

Gigi Argyropoulou, for example, discusses the practice of "dislocating" as a working method of engaging with a particular context while simultaneously moving away from it to shift, shake, or break existing patterns of thought and perception. The goal is to bring perspectives "from below" into play against existing institutional hierarchies. Her example of the Teatro Valle in Rome illustrates that new legal forms can also be developed in this process, ones that preserve the ethos of public participation and promote processes of "commoning." It is also about transformative strategies that allow for new forms of collaboration based on "friendships" in collapsed and ephemeral infrastructures.

Maria Hlavajova emphasizes the process of constant searching and restarting in which the institution is questioned and reconstituted through critical imagination. The central actor of these processes is a "radical audience" that cannot be reduced to countable "visitors" in the sense of neoliberal logics. They are actors who help to shape the institution in a permanent process of approaching and distancing, transcending existing orders of space and time. The separation of the local and the global is replaced by a critical situatedness that permanently shifts the demarcation between the internal and external depending on the problem at hand. Instead of traditional utopian concepts of the future, it is a matter of locating the "not-yet existing" in the concrete practice of anticipatory learning for the purpose of radical justice. In aesthetically social forms of improvisation, ways of life that are worth living can be practiced collectively.

The practice of Forensic Architecture presented by Eyal Weizman exposes state-sanctioned human rights violations using a counter-forensics that redirects our view from the victim to the perpetrator. The forensics of state institutions are countered by a forensics based on participatory methods of investigation combined with aesthetic and scientific procedures, which thereby introduce diverse perspectives that are often deliberately excluded in the official narrative. Through close collaboration with the affected communities, an alternative counter-knowledge to the existing knowledge of domination emerges. In this way, Forensic Architecture attacks the monopoly on truth of state institutions and their enforcing of belief by means of traditional authority. At the same time, however, it also resists the relativization of post-truth theories—a denial of reality in which crimes can no longer be prosecuted—and "alternative facts," a logic through which state authority is often merely replaced by demagogic authority. The success of counter-forensics hinges on replacing a rigid concept of truth with the concept of verification. The credibility of verification is not enforced by an existing institution but is established through a procedure that involves as many perspectives as possible in a social and epistemological process.

The contributions presented so far deal with para-institutional forms of thought and action as counter-models to existing power relations. However, if there is too much power asymmetry between the interlocutors, one side is silenced, as Adania Shibli shows in her essay. This can be a resigned, intimidated, reactive silencing, but it can also be a political act that excludes the powerful from their own communication.

Olaf Nicolai's images of graphs and clouds round out the volume, pointing to the two sides that play a fundamental role in the development of new forms of thought and action and thus also language: that is, imagination and methodological procedure.

Bernd Scherer

Translated from the German by Faith Ann Gibson

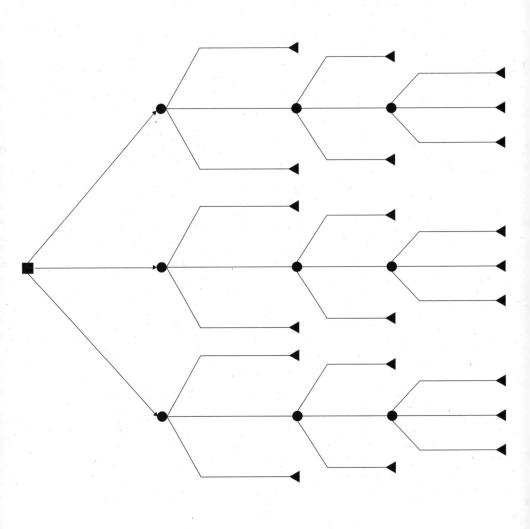

Instituting Otherwise:
Ten Observations "With-Within-Against"[1]

1. A friend once confided in me that he was concerned about the disquieting restlessness—this constant push and pull and ongoing stream of demands, as he perceived it—in the way the "radical publics" interacted with BAK, basis voor actuele kunst.[2] After all, isn't BAK driven by the same urgencies of the disastrous present as these very publics? By a deep disenchantment with the conditions of the collapsing world? By a yearning to put into practice, in both art and life, the principles of social, cultural, and ecological justice? Why then was there such a challenging, strained relationship?

My friend, speaking from a relatively "conventional" cultural experience, namely from working with a renowned ensemble—a relatively homogenous group of mostly western and just-about-well-off musicians (albeit hanging onto the middle-class denominator by a thin thread), dedicated to the repertoire of one certain eighteenth-century composer—said he had experienced none of that with their audience. "But wait," he then mused offhandedly and in an accidentally revelatory manner, "even as we're playing to full concert halls and appreciative

1   I borrow the phrase "with-within-against" from Athena Athanasiou, "Performing the Institution 'As If It Were Possible,'" in Maria Hlavajova and Simon Sheikh (eds), *Former West: Art and the Contemporary After 1989*. Cambridge, MA and Utrecht: MIT Press and BAK, 2016, p. 683.

2   In this essay I speak from within, and at times "with-within-against" BAK, basis voor actuele kunst, Utrecht—a base for art, theory, and social action that is committed to the notion of art as a public sphere and a political space and to aesthetico-political experimentations with and through art—where, as its founding artistic director, I have been fortunate to work since its inception in 2000. The observations in this text come from an ongoing collective engagement with art and life through BAK's institutional lens, driven by the urgencies of the world today. The word "collective" is of critical importance here: in full acknowledgement of the inter- and ultra-dependences that are *our* only way to live more justly and more completely, I want to acknowledge that the ideas in this text emerged from multiple conversations within the community "with-within-against" BAK, which I have been privileged to enjoy and can now share. With special thanks to Jeanne van Heeswijk and all colleagues at BAK, as well as to Aidan Wall for their thoughts and the wonderful suggestions they made on this text.

audiences, could it be that without any demands truly being made on us that, actually, . . . we don't matter?"

The fleeting inkling about irrelevance and an either-this-or-that worldview aside, it made me wonder. Namely, about whether, for a public art institution to practice meaningfully in (spite of) the world today,[3] it presupposes not an audience, but a demanding community of cultural practices and forms of life—indeed, *radical publics*,[4] for lack of a better term—to hold it relentlessly "under pressure" and to account.

2. To hold the institution to account by its publics, if persistently and uncompromisingly, is not simply for the sake of opposing it. The complex relationality at play disbands with the false binary that has long colonized the institutional imagination of my generation: that one has a choice, either to work *inside* the institution or *outside* of it. The latter stance—coalescing around attitudes of anti-institutional resistance and efforts to categorically separate from (state-)public infrastructure—has materialized in a particularly disorienting and exhausting variant of institutional critique. This variant traffics in artistic experimentation predominantly between artists or cultural practitioners and institutions. In its glorification of individual bohemian rebellion, if I dare say so—which is not to be confused with any form of social change—it prevents radical imaginaries from seeping out of artistic and intellectual enclosures, and thus thwarts the possibility of their potential actualization in and across multiple lifeworlds. Even though this version of institutional critique often produces powerful discourse, it also often churns out, to put it somewhat bluntly, powerless politics. Correspondingly, it often initiates celebrated artworks—habitually included in the art collections of the very institutions their makers have critically engaged with—as much as it often produces a so-called "weak public" of onlookers without access to either policy-making or public

3 For the sake of brevity, I refer to the "public art institution" as "institution" for the remainder of this essay.

4 I use the term "radical publics" for lack of a better term to grasp the various reorientations away from the commonplace notion of "the audience." By "radical," I point to their advocating for social, cultural, and ecological justice, grasping the problems at their "roots" as the etymological origin of the word, *radicalis*, suggests.

decisions,[5] and thus also with little political accountability. By definition a rhetorical, critical-discursive, and opinion-forming practice, when equating "agency" solely with anti-institutional resistance, it inevitably lacks pathways to the public governance it covets—to shaping public life, if you will.

The challenge this situation opens up is one of how to sustain critical work vis-à-vis the institution *and* concurrently prevent it from drawing inhibiting borderlines around itself. There must be new possibilities for understanding and practicing the institution differently—as a *situated*, *embodied*, and *relational* proposition of another politics.

3. Overcoming the habits of mere aversion to the institution, a strategy for the radical publics I have observed is to hold the institution to account by pressuring it to "*always* newly start again."[6] This is not a labor of contestation over the institution per se, but rather of the course of the gradual, sclerotic regimentation of the (state-)administrative power mechanisms that every institution sets out toward, albeit at different speeds and scales, from the very point of its inception. In other words, this is not a spectacle of institutional critique, but an opening up to a politics that at the same time *resists* and *enacts* the institution through critical *imagination-as-practice*. This process engages simultaneously disruption and sustainability, closeness and detachment, movement and transition through a succession of interconnected "instituent" events. In this case, these are events that interpolate artistic and discursive enclosures in (and of) the institution with practical, tactical, and concrete exigencies of the crisis-ridden present. This is no less than a collective, public practice of institution making—of what I have called *instituting otherwise*.

5   See Nancy Fraser, "Rethinking the Public Sphere: A Contribution to the Critique of Actually Existing Democracy," in Craig Calhoun (ed.), *Habermas and the Public Sphere*. Cambridge, MA: MIT Press, 1992, pp. 107-42.

6   In a similar vein—albeit with an example of the institution as the common rather than the public art institution, as is the case in this essay—philosopher and art theorist Gerald Raunig speaks of "instituent practices" as those which do not oppose the institution but escape institutionalization. See Gerald Raunig, "Flatness Rules: Instituent Practices and Institutions of the Common in a Flat World," in Pascal Gielen (ed.), *Institutional Attitudes: Instituting Art in a Flat World*. Amsterdam: Valiz, 2013, pp. 167-78.

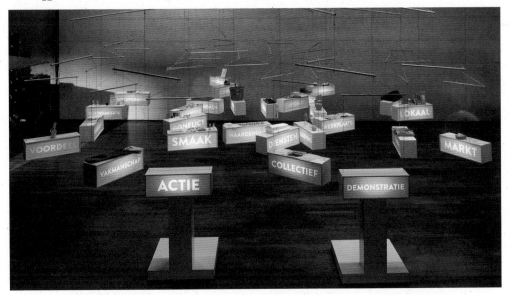

Trainings for the Not-Yet, BAK, 2019–2020. Jeanne van Heeswijk and Afrikaanderwijk Cooperative, *Mobile of Interdependency (Acts of Balance)*, 2014. Photo: Tom Janssen

4. Instituting otherwise—always ongoing, always searching, always incomplete—is thus a relational practice of de-institutionalizing and consequently re-institutionalizing into a framework for rehearsing life that resists hegemonic paradigms. This is done not merely through critique, but through proposition and (re-)invention of *ourselves* within a more just world. As the frame emerges in the transversal overlaps of multiple stakeholders—the (progressive) institution, politically driven cultural practices, and other social actors (social movements and political activism, for example)—it collectively models a "future practice" of "the production and treatment of political-aesthetic problem complexes."[7]

5. Radical publics, this agglomeration of cultural-social practices and actors,[8] is an entity decidedly different from the commonplace under-

---

7   Ibid., p. 175.

8   This notion of radical publics does away with how, under the aegis of western modernity, the field of art—or the institution of art—has been conventionally apportioned into the triad of the artist, the institution, and the audience. Radical publics—radical artistic and cultural practices plus other social actors—is not merely external, but may be, to a certain extent, internal to the day-to-day life of the institution, facilitating temporary, transversal, and tactical coalitions with various "stakeholders" and "users." This pertains to institutions that themselves emerged from philosophy and practice of institutional critique (the "institutional-critique institutions," as it were). Raunig argues (again, in his plea for "the institution of the common," that it is thinkable that "the institutional critique in the narrower sense, in other words the critique of production conditions in the cultural field and critique of concrete institutions, will be conducted in the best case by the institution of the common itself." See ibid., p. 176. Advancing this proposition to overcome the institutional-critique practice that aims to merely "reassess or renew working conditions and visibility in the space of art," art theorist Marina Vishmidt offers a term "infrastructural critique." Here, the ambition of infrastructural critique is social (rather than simply artistic) transformation, for which it "signals a view of the art institution as a site of resources—material and symbolic—and [...] calls for an opportunist deployment for the sake of furthering all sorts of projects rather than the loyal criticism attendant on 'institutional critique' in its established version." See Marina Vishmidt, "Beneath the Atelier, the Desert: Critique, Institutional and Infrastructural," in Maria Hlavajova and Tom Holert (eds), *Marion von Osten: Once We Were Artists (A BAK Critical Reader in Artists' Practice)*. Amsterdam and Utrecht: Valiz and BAK, 2017, p. 222.

standing of the so-called audience.[9] The audience—let's envisage it simply, for the sake of this argument, as comprised of the modalities of the viewer, spectator, observer, consumer, client, or even partici- pant[10]—has been designed to match the patronizing institutional log- ic of incorporation of ever-newer, ever-larger, ever-more creative in- dividuals into the ideology of western (colonial, capitalist, extractivist) modernity. Fitted into the quantitative-economic argument as much as the neoliberal creative imperative,[11] the audience,[12] so understood, is then subsumed by institutional technology that is geared toward keeping alive the bourgeois version of culture in all its gendered,

9   See also Maria Hlavajova and Ranjit Hoskote (eds), *Future Publics (The Rest Can and Should Be Done by the People): A Critical Reader in Contemporary Art*. Amsterdam and Utrecht: Valiz and BAK, 2015.

10   Despite the agreeable "warmth" around the notion of participation, I am of a belief that institutions often show an embarrassing weakness when they stage participation as a "democratic right" to take part in culture through the roles and protocols they prescribe, all the while wrongfully monopolizing the notion of culture as a commodity they trade in. Through such scripted, mechanical attempts disguised as the "democratization of culture," the participation imperative, which once may have sought transparency and inclusion, today is divested of its emancipatory origins. To truly "take part," thus, cannot be equated with following the pathways of controlled access to the grand schemes of the institution, but rather of engaging in the collaborative processes within the unforeseeable relational field of forces that do away with predefined roles and rules. This notion of participation is driven by a yearning to overcome these very institutionally-guarded inequalities and power differentials among "authors," "users," or "stakeholders," to say the least. Participation "organizes" in a de-authorized manner, rhizomatically, and without a center.

11   Granted, both these ideas of "culture for all" and "culture from all," which underwrite the pleas for access and universal creativity respectively, once considered progressive, have cultivated their twisted alter egos under the aegis of neoliberal capitalism, leading to the habits of populist quantification and to the obligation of individual creativity.

12   One exception, however, argued by curator and writer Simon Sheikh, is worth considering in relation to the institutions, as "the very word 'audience' also has its semantic double: audience not as spectators or listeners, but audience as something granted by power," which opens a pathway to thinking of institutions as places where such encounters with power can be brokered. See Simon Sheikh, "A Long Walk to the Land of the People: Contemporary Art in the Spectre of Spectatorship," in Hlavajova and Hoskote (eds), *Future Publics*, pp. 230-61.

Trainings for the Not-Yet, BAK, 2019–2020. Philadelphia Assembled and Jeanne van Heeswijk, *Toward Sanctuary Dome*, 2017. Photo: Tom Janssen

classed, ethnic, and racial articulations that rigidify the extant world of ruthless injustices while manufacturing new ones. In this orthodoxy, the institution is to "provide" its audience access to high culture: mainly the artistic treasures and colonial troves conserved alongside the logic of canonization, spectacularization, and universalization of select cultural products.

But the radical publics are not up for grabs for the institution as mere visitor-number statistics, for they resist the policies of cooptation described above, doing so by continuously renegotiating power and agency in a series of push and pull interactions. Even though the institution is always already implicated in the production of inequalities that drive the radical publics in the first place, instituting otherwise presupposes that there is a *possibility* and a shared *commitment* to pursue the relational modalities of solidarity, coalitionality, and even accompliceship. If access, too, is at stake for radical publics—instead of cultural spoils, or their ability to "participate" in "culture" that is propagated as expert knowledge and severed from locally embedded social life—it concerns access to a yet-to-be-realized *livable life in common.*

6. Feminist social anthropologist Athena Athanasiou addressed the ethical and political underpinnings of such relationality vis-à-vis the institution as being "with-within-against."[13] This position facilitates the tactics of an "uncanny occupation" of the institution,[14] acknowledging that as much as the institutions destroy us, they sustain us at the same time.[15] The "with-within-against," then, this "spectral political location of both proximity and distance," allows one "to de-authorize the institution's normalizing violence,"[16] even if temporarily, while simultaneously defending it against "neoliberal de-institutionalization," as the contemporary fascist forces take hold of the present conjuncture.[17] For indeed, even though institutions are deeply "im-

---

13 Athanasiou, "Performing the Institution 'As If It Were Possible,'" p. 683.
14 Ibid.
15 Even though the notion of "we" and "us" is sensitive, and one must be aware that the institutions do destroy and sustain "us" to different degrees, the yearning for "us" and another "world" is constitutive of this argument.
16 Athanasiou, "Performing the Institution 'As If It Were Possible,'" p. 683.
17 Ibid., p. 684.

plicated in our suffering," we *do* need them; we do urgently need "public spaces, homes, parks, schools, hospitals, libraries, and art institutions," because, through "their commitment to public interest," they contain the *prospect* of "living and being-in-common."[18]

7. This prospective temporality, to be sure, must disengage from the violent mockery of life in the necropolitics wedded to western linear time. Upholding the neoliberal capitalist utopia alongside its abstract flow, it outsources life to an unknown future on a yet-to-be-colonized island populated by a yet-to-be-discovered human species, who— *unbelievably!*—no longer wage wars. In reality, this hegemonic futurity—disguised as a promise of redemption, to which it directs our hopes—extorts in the now unspeakable structural injustices and deaths due to poverty, racialization, heteronormativity, or "just" bombs falling. I am now also writing to (only seemingly) distant sounds of warfare destroying all that is in its way—human and nonhuman, living and nonliving, organic and nonorganic—in Ukraine, but also in Ethiopia, Yemen, Palestine, and many, too many, other places across the planet.

To recast the institution away from the grand utopian narrative of the modern politics of time—that is synonymous with an infinite concatenation of disasters—one must actively desert its defuturing doctrine. Essentially a labor of decolonizing time, such desertion from the universal clock calls for a creative reinvention of another chronopolitics: one that drafts a pathway to a futurity that circumnavigates both the utopianism of hope and the negativism of despair.

Let us think and act along the contours of *the not-yet.*[19]

---

18 Ibid., p. 683.

19 This notion links to artist Jeanne van Heeswijk's influential thinking and practicing of "the not-yet." She has been developing this notion across multiple projects, including in intensive collaboration with BAK in *Trainings for the Not-Yet*, "an exhibition as a series of trainings for a future of being together otherwise," which took place at BAK (2019–20); in a consequent publication (Jeanne van Heeswijk, Maria Hlavajova, and Rachael Rakes (eds), *Toward the Not-Yet: Art as Public Practice.* Cambridge, MA and Utrecht: MIT Press and BAK, 2021); culminating in our current collaborative rethinking of BAK from art institution to "community portal."

Trainings for the Not-Yet, BAK, 2019–2020. Training with artist
Patricia Kaersenhout, *(New) Formats of Care in Times of Violence*.
Photo: Tom Janssen

The politico-temporal model of the not-yet is guided by the vision that it is not only necessary but possible to restore to life—as well as to epistemological and aesthetic practices—the notions of radical equity and justice collectively and without deferral. *Time plus praxis*, or better yet, *time plus space plus agency*, is its formula, to borrow for this the words of the social and political theorist Omedi Ochieng. At stake is "the radical politics of ungovernability"—consisting of collectively practicing, against all odds, in the here and now—and "a radical, comprehensive, nuanced, and multidimensional imagination about what ultimately makes for a good society."[20]

For the institution, to run on the not-yet's time means to meet the possibility of proposition, prefiguration, and pre-enactment, and offer itself as a *portal*, as it were, to an *elsewhen*—and thus to another politics.

8. What about the *elsewhere*? Considering that linear time goes hand in hand with a particular understanding of geography (and thus geopolitics), the spatial fixity undergirding the institution's practices needs to undergo a series of reorientations and disruptions to inhabit the not-yet. The practice of radicalizing the local,[21] in the interaction with radical publics, is paramount in this process, for it enacts the non-capitalist relationality of being together in spite of the neoliberal politico-economic imperative of the present. Yet, the notion of radicalizing the local—although embedded in concrete community—also

20 Omedi Ochieng, "Chronotopia; Imagination, Social Change, and Justice in African Social Movements," lecture, Texas Lutheran University, Texas (April 10, 2011), https://www.youtube.com/watch?v=h1AI7z-Wu9A; see also Omedi Ochieng, "Utopianism, Anti-Utopianism, and the Radical Politics of Chronotopian Ungovernability," in conversation with Rachael Rakes at BAK, basis voor actuele kunst, Utrecht, as part of *Fragments of Repair/Gathering III* (May 13, 2021), https://www.youtube.com/watch?v=SEUiRT_7z6M&t=1652s, both accessed September 18, 2022.

21 The notion of "radicalizing the local" borrows from the work of van Heeswijk and her multitude of collaborations in the city, and with the Afrikaanderwijk Cooperative in particular, *Freehouse: Radicalizing the Local* (2008-ongoing), which reflects the struggle for the right to live well in the Afrikaanderwijk neighborhood of Rotterdam. The cooperative has sought neighborhood empowerment through community participation, cultural and economic self-organization, and inclusive urban development.

detaches the idea of locality from its simplified zip-code identity by actively enmeshing it with similar affective and political practices elsewhere. By extension, it detaches the local from the exhausting contestations of the "global" engagement it has grappled with over the last three or so decades.

If art has been complicit with both the modern and the global,[22] the local has long been understood to function as a site of resistance to neoliberal globalization and its violence, prioritizing communities and environment over the circulation of art commodities within the circuit of museum to biennale to free-port storage vault. Today, however, the local sadly resists globalization equally with xenophobia and populist nationalism, offering not a livable political alternative, but rather a deepening of the world disorder by reflecting global violence in the countless pieces of broken mirror in its own backyard. This is not to disregard the extant local, indigenous strategies of resistance— these are critical in instituting otherwise—but rather, to work out collectively how to meet the challenge through an invention that thrives *in spite of* (rather than "merely" *against*) the morbid symptoms of the present. Thinking the elsewhere to globalization today might thus go along with the epistemic and ontological shift away from the imagined binary of local versus global, and embody instead critical *situatedness*.[23] Deposed from the idealized positions of global and local, or universal and particular, situatedness frustrates the power differentials by which these positions are produced. Situatedness engages neither a separate geography nor an all-in-the-world-encompassing global ambition, rather it employs the relational affective and ideological modalities driven by urgencies that may replicate across topologies of different sorts: across varied localities, times, practices, and movements. This allows for thinking, imagining, and acting otherwise,

22 Undoubtedly, contemporary art can be understood as an ideological and iconographic source of neoliberal globalization and, following philosopher Fredric Jameson, even as the cultural logic of globalization.

23 The idea of situatedness in this essay draws from philosopher Donna Haraway's notion of "situated knowledges." See Donna Haraway, "Situated Knowledges: The Science Question in Feminism and the Privilege of Partial Perspective," *Feminist Studies*, vol. 14, no. 3 (Autumn, 1988), pp. 575-99.

Trainings for the Not-Yet, BAK, 2019–2020. Training with artist
Patricia Kaersenhout, *(New) Formats of Care in Times of Violence*.
Photo: Tom Janssen

elsewhen, and with similarly situated elsewheres in building a terrestrial community of praxis.[24] Imagining the institution situated in, say, a social movement—simultaneously here and elsewhere, now and *elsewhen*—rather than in the circuits of global domination or local resistance, it offers a vista of another way of being together. It shows a form of relationship based on transversal and heterogeneous connections—among different struggles, different institutions, different networks, different intensities, and different durations.[25] This is a process of de-institutionalization and re-institutionalization, again, dispersed into an ex-centric coalition of a multisited grid of practices. Breaking from the traditional means of time–space homogeneity through centrifugal forces, it is a form of institution with no "inside" or "outside"—an *extitution* to come.[26]

9. What is the role of such an extitution, really? *Anticipatory learning*, I hazard: a coming together to learn what does not yet exist.

Concerned with publicness, anticipatory learning is less a pedagogy *for* or *of* the public than a pedagogy that *enacts publicly* the political potential of relational processes that are fully committed to equality and justice. It is—again—a form of disruption. A disruption of the "normal" order of things so as to create an asynchronous, unaligned time–space from which the rational, predetermined, and policed roles and rules are removed, and which thus makes it possible

---

24 I use the term terrestrial, which is neither global nor trans-/international, in order to circumvent the reliance on geopolitical denominators in need of undoing, whether it is the nation-state, an agglomeration of nation-states, or the notion of the global absorbed by the neoliberal doctrine that took over the original meaning of "worldwide."

25 The BAK Fellowship for Situated Practice has been experimenting with the potentials of the extitution since 2021 in a program consisting of four interconnected research cells that engage with situated contexts of complex, interrelated histories and the nows of colonialism and labor migration, among other urgencies. Working alongside the BAK-based cell are: the GUDsel, hosted by GUDSKUL, Jakarta; the Istanbul cell, hosted by the Istanbul Biennial Production and Research Programme at Istanbul Foundation for Culture and Arts (IKSV), Istanbul; and the Cell for Digital Discomfort, consisting of cultural practitioners working predominantly in an online environment.

26 See Michel Serres, *Atlas*. Julliard: Paris, 1994.

for people to come into the company of others as *themselves*.[27] This "infinitely improbable" form of being together[28]—one that is *not yet* though already *situated* across concrete struggles—cannot be planned or known in advance. Despite its unavailability in so-called reality, it nonetheless intuits a political sensibility of a world otherwise.

To learn collectively what does not yet exist means to both construct and inhabit the space of fiction, scaffolded along the politics of the world *we* want. It thus also means to appeal to the at one time key faculty of art and culture to radically imagine the aesthetic lifeworlds that extend into the unknowable. Learning to circumvent representation and face the limits of critique, it also rewrites the idea of art as resistance into *re-existence*: a space to rehearse a livable life in common.[29] Yet, just as it appeals to strangeness and things not-yet-familiar, it also sends ripples back into the here and now, against all odds, to enthuse the present with a sense of possibility. Anticipatory learning, born out of disruption, produces dissensus and heterogeneity, and thus, it can only thrive in and build upon disagreement.

10. This extitution, one could argue, is an invention; it is not yet. But it *is* in the making in many situated contexts and times around the globe—always ongoing, always searching, always incomplete. It is evolving through aesthetico-social improvisation in constant motion—fugitive, organized and self-organized, and always collective.

If, together with the radical publics, the institution can be recast into a "community portal," as mentioned above, I imagine it as a space that can render inactive the chronopolitics of the present—even if only temporarily—so as to pave a way for wondrous incoming elsewheres,

---

27 This proposition builds on Gert Biesta's theory of a "pedagogy of interruption" and its further interpretation, based on examples of artistic practice (including that of van Heeswijk), by Arthur Caris and Gillian Cowell. See Gert Biesta, "Becoming public: Public pedagogy, citizenship and the public sphere," *Social and Cultural Geography*, vol. 13, no. 7 (2012), pp. 683-97; and Arthur Caris and Gillian Cowell, "The Artist Can't Escape: The Artist as (Reluctant) Public Pedagogue," *Policy Futures in Education*, vol. 14, no. 4 (2016), pp. 466-83.

28 See Ibid., p. 472, quoting from Biesta, "Becoming public."

29 With thanks to Rolando Vázquez for introducing artist and anthropologist Adolfo Albán Achinte's concept of "re-existence" during his talk at BAK.

extitution

beneath

elsewhens, and otherwises. And as this knowledge meets the real through the residue one carries back with them into the everyday, it is there, to be sure, that the prospect of another world will appear. Just imagine what an extitution can do through its multiplicity.

Instituting otherwise, then, is less about the institution than it is about helping to create the conditions for thinking through, imagining, and living that imagination to actualize ways of *being together otherwise*. It is a practice of worldmaking, but more than that, it is a possibility to rehearse livable life in common. This is of critical importance no doubt, for, in the words of the educator, writer, public scholar, and spoken word artist Walidah Imarisha, "we can't build what we can't imagine."[30]

30 Walidah Imarisha, "To Build a Future Without Police and Prisons, We have to Imagine It First," *OneZero* (October 22, 2020), https://onezero. medium.com/black-lives-matter-is-science-fiction-how-envisioning-a-better-future-makes-it-possible-5e14d35154e3#:~:text=To%20Build%20 a%20Future%20Without,First%20%7C%20by%20Walidah%20 Imarisha%20%7C%20OneZero, accessed September 19, 2022.

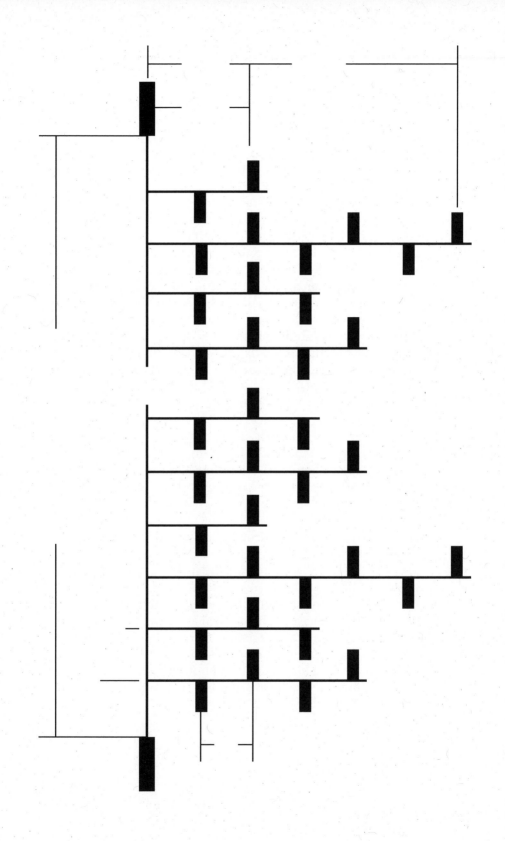

Attempts at Destituting a Language, Instituting Another

Jerusalem. Late 2000. I head to the post office with a box I want to send overseas. In the post office, I go to stand in a line. I no longer care how long I will have to wait. Waiting, in Palestine, has become a lifestyle.

There are three people ahead of me and I am taking shelter inside my silence. I read all the advertisements posted up in the place. There is a little girl clinging to her mother's blue dress. She stares at me shamelessly. Sometimes she stands on one foot while her mouth moves as if humming a song that she has just improvised, but which is voiceless. She only moves her lips, and stares at the box and at me. Her mother whispers in the ear of another woman beside her, and I do not know if she too is in the line. If so, there would be four in front of me. In front of them are a man and his daughter; she paces up and down the post office and then returns to her father and whispers in his ear.

Later, a new woman joins us.

Most of the people standing in the line are Palestinians. The only Israeli is at the head. His voice fills the space with an American-accented Hebrew, while the others whisper. They look around them and comment on things in whispers.

And mine—if I speak when I reach the teller, how will my voice come out? I try to imagine my voice. I rehearse its melody in my head. I will speak in English. Will I say hello, or get straight to the subject?

The two little girls look at me and I do not know why. I do not want to smile at them. They continue to look at me, especially the one in front of me. I look back at her, and at length, then I notice a glimpse of fear in her eyes, and my eyes fill with tears on realizing that I'm the source of the fear she feels.

I lower my eyes, and a teardrop falls off my nose to the floor between my feet. The little girl continues to look at me.

The Israeli leaves. The man with the little girl approaches and says in a quiet, hesitant voice, in Hebrew and in Arabic and in all that is available, that he wants to withdraw everything he has in his account. The teller says in a clear and neutral Hebrew that she does not have enough money in the cash register. He does not understand, and she repeats the same sentence. He continues standing silently. He then asks the two women in front of me about what she has said. They say they do not know Hebrew. One of them says maybe that woman knows, pointing at the woman behind me. This one says she knows a little bit and she moves forward. Slowly and with a lot of effort and whispering, she tries to ask the teller what she has said.

They did not turn to me. I do not help them because they did not turn to me. I know Hebrew, but I do not help them. I am silent. I hear all their efforts and remain silent.

I am not one hundred percent sure that the teller is racist, but fear she is. I am afraid that my box will not arrive at its desired destination on time, if she realizes that I am a Palestinian. She will neglect it; she will forget it for weeks. It will not receive the same care other non-Arab boxes receive. Now I take cover behind my silence. I do not open my mouth. I can feel very well my teeth in my closed jaws. I justify it by telling myself that no one has turned to me. I am hiding my Arabness. At the same time, I cannot take my eyes away from the scene. I follow it, follow their efforts, follow their hesitant whispered words, follow my denial of them. I wish I would speak no more. I wish I had spoken seconds ago. But I am silent. I remain silent.[1]

Silence

The phenomenon of Palestinians taking refuge in silence whenever they are around Hebrew speakers in Palestine/Israel to avoid being discriminated against, even verbally or physically attacked, is not an unfamiliar one. As a matter of fact, almost every Palestinian who was born after 1948, after the creation of the state of Israel, has had to undergo this experience at least once in their lifetime. Decades of Zionist colonization and Israeli military occupation has made speaking in Arabic a fraught experience; one that may not necessarily signify a simple act of communication where one can only expect a corresponding answer. Once a Palestinian speaks in Arabic in the proximity of Israelis, thereby revealing their identity, they can expect to be the subject of discrimination and sometimes of attacks. A news article published in the Israeli daily newspaper *Haaretz* reports on just such an instance:

> Dozens of Jewish youths attacked three young Palestinians in Jerusalem's Zion Square early on Friday morning [...].

1   The opening section of this essay was translated from the Arabic to English by Yasmine Hannoush.

One of the Palestinians was seriously wounded and hospital-
ized in intensive care [...].

> The three were allegedly attacked by youths shouting
'Death to the Arabs' at them, as well as other racial slurs. One
of them fell on the floor, and his attackers continued to beat
him until he lost consciousness.

> [...]

[R]escue volunteers and [...] services arrived on the scene and
found the victim with no pulse and not breathing. After a lengthy
resuscitation attempt, he was transferred to the hospital.

> Writing on her Facebook page, one eyewitness described
the attack as a lynch: 'today I saw a lynch with my own eyes [...]
dozens of youths ran and gathered and started to really beat to
death three Arab youths.'[2]

It could be said nowadays that the experience of Palestinians speaking Arabic in Israel/Palestine is totally opposite to the case of Shahrazad (Scheherazade) in *One Thousand and One Nights*. There, Shahrazad needed to keep speaking; never to be silent, in order to postpone
her own death. Speaking was simply her guarantee that she would not
be killed. Edward Said elaborates on this, saying that *One Thousand
and One Nights* establishes the continuous human voice as an assur-
ance of the continuity of human life, whereas silence is associated with
death. Said writes:

> [A]s in the case of Shahrazad, she can prolong life not only by
> reciting her marvelous tales but also by physically producing
> a new generation. This she does in the course of her immense-
> ly long narration: we learn from the concluding frame that she
> has had three sons whom she brings to Shahriar [...] and the
> couple and their children live on happily ever after.[3]

---

2   Nir Hasson, "In Suspected Jerusalem Lynch, Dozens of Jewish Youths
    Attack 3 Palestinians," *Haaretz* (August 17, 2012), https://www.haaretz.
    com/suspected-lynch-in-jerusalem-1.5286138, accessed September 25,
    2022.
3   Edward W. Said, *Reflections on Exile and Other Essays*. London: Granta
    Books, 1997, pp. 474–75.

What was the process by which silence, rather than speaking, got introduced into the lives of Palestinians as a tool to guarantee their survival, opposite to Shahrazad's recital in *One Thousand and One Nights*?

One answer can be found in an essay by historian Rana Barakat, titled "To Un-Mute Silence," where she refers to silence in its verb form, as in "silencing":

> Silencing has a long and varied story in Palestine. Silence's colonial verbal connotation can be traced back to the denial of peoplehood in the text of the mandate imposed on Palestine and Palestinians after the First World War. The European conquerors from Britain in their formal text of governance named indigenous people of Palestine: 'non-Jews.' Negation is a partner of silencing, and denial and silencing are companions, whom the settlers brought together.
>
> From the time of un-naming Palestinians at the beginning of British colonial rule in Palestine, silencing's predilection to settlers has been the dominant story in Palestine for over a century [...]. In this long history, silencing is surely a partner with repression. Silencing and repression [...] are the settler fantasy couple.[4]

Silence and silencing are political maneuvers introduced by the colonizers, as the poet Aimé Césaire reminds us in his seminal text *Discourse on Colonialism*. Rather than elevating the non-Western world, the colonizers decivilized the colonized by silencing them. As such, the act of silencing is essential to the process of colonization, because it eliminates the past existence of the colonized peoples; it becomes as unworthy of mention as their history and culture.[5] This has been the story of Palestinians under British rule, and later under Israeli occupation. Furthermore, silencing dictates the type of relationship the colonizers have with the colonized. By rendering them silent, in the main the colonized would be seen (i.e. as objects) and rarely heard (i.e.

4   Rana Barakat, "To Un-Mute Silence," *28 Magazine*, no. 12 (2018), pp. 136–44, here pp. 138–39 (in Arabic).
5   Aimé Césaire, *Discourse on Colonialism*. New York: Monthly Review Press, 2001.

as human subjects). This typically implies that in "looking," the focus is on behavior. Voiceless, devoid of access to language and reason, irrationality and sometimes delinquency would be attributed by the colonizer to the actions and even the culture of the colonized, which the former considered irrational, uncivilized, violent.

Colonialism does not only express contempt toward the history and culture of the colonized by silencing both, it shows contempt for their language as well. On July 19, 2018, the Israeli government—led by a nationalist right-wing and Jewish religious coalition—passed a new law, known as the Nationality Law. This law defines Israel as the nation-state of the Jewish people, and sets out "the development of Jewish settlements nationwide as a national priority."[6] Furthermore, the law strips Arabic of its designation as an official language in Israel/Palestine alongside Hebrew, and downgrades it to a "special status."[7]

Arabic, however, had been downgraded from an official language to a threat long ago. A story told to me by a friend who lives in Jerusalem reveals how some Israelis have casually come to perceive the Arabic language in recent years. The story dates to early 2015, during the Israeli election campaign taking place at the time. My friend—in an exaggeratedly frightened voice that, by lowering it at times, was almost caricature-like—described how:

> On my way to work one morning, just before the Israeli elections, I saw from a distance an Egged Bus,[8] with Arabic writing on the back. I couldn't believe my eyes. What? An Israeli bus with Arabic writing over it? Is Arabic language being displayed so clearly and openly and so big? I thought I was imagining what I was seeing. This can't be true. I immediately changed my route, and followed that bus. I drove faster and faster to catch up with it to see what was written in Arabic on the back.
>
> Finally, as I got closer to the bus, I saw underneath the Arabic a line written in Hebrew saying, 'If you don't vote for

---

6   Israeli Knesset, *Basic-Law—Israel: The Nation State of the Jewish People*,
     2018, https://knesset.gov.il/laws/special/eng/BasicLawNationState.pdf,
     accessed October 13, 2018.
7   Ibid.
8   Egged is the region's largest local and inter-city Israeli-run public bus
     company.

the Jewish Home party, you will see this language everywhere and not only in this ad.'

Until a few years ago, the leader of the Jewish Home party was Israeli Minister of Education Naftali Bennett, a member of the last Israeli government. Bennett had been the Israeli Prime Minister from June 2021 to June 2022.

Arabic In and Out of Palestine

In his memoir *Out of Place*, Edward Said recalls the status of the Arabic language in Palestine, and accordingly in his life, prior to the creation of the state of Israel in 1948, before he and his family were forced to leave Jerusalem, where they lived. Said, who attended his first year of school in Jerusalem, writes:

> Our daily conversation in school and home was uniformly in Arabic; unlike in Cairo, where English was encouraged, our family in Jerusalem 'belonged' and our native language prevailed everywhere.[9]

Said, as the quote implies, arrived in Cairo, Egypt, after 1948. In Egypt, which was then occupied by the British, Arabic was allowed minimal presence in his formative education. In *Out of Place*, he goes on to describe some of the efforts to silence Arabic in his life, starting in the first years of his education in English, at American and British-run Schools in Cairo. In "a little pamphlet entitled 'The School Handbook,'" Said writes, "Rule 1 stated categorically: English is the language of the school. Anyone caught speaking other languages will be severely punished."[10]

He continues:

> Being and speaking Arabic were delinquent activities at Victoria College, and accordingly we were never given proper instruction in our own language, history, culture, and geography. We were

9   Edward W. Said, *Out of Place: A Memoir*. New York: Vintage Books, 2000/1999, pp. 253–54.
10   Ibid., p. 420.

tested as if we were English boys, trailing behind an ill-defined and always out-of-reach goal from class to class, year to year [...]. I knew in my heart that Victoria College had irreversibly severed my links with my old life, [...] and that we all felt that we were inferiors pitted against a wounded colonial power, that was dangerous and capable of inflicting harm on us, even as we seemed compelled to study its language and its culture as the dominant one in Egypt.[11]

To some extent, here, Said reveals the effects of linguistic repression and alienation in the formation of his thought and writing, where his knowledge of the Arabic language, of Arabic history, culture, and geography, were marginalized. As such, his writings can in part be understood in connection with his sense of alienation, of the silencing he endured early on in his life.

Said was equally aware of the workings of this linguistic alienation and its causes in the wider context, and not only in his personal life. A decade or so before writing *Out of Place*, he wrote an essay titled "Goodbye to Mahfooz":

For of all the major literatures and languages, Arabic is by far the least known and the most grudgingly regarded by Europeans and Americans, a huge irony given that all Arabs regard the immense literary and cultural worth of their language as one of their principal contributions to the world. Arabic [...] has a hieratic, historical and everyday use that is almost without parallel in other world cultures. Because of that role, and because it has always been associated with resistance to the imperialist incursions that have characterised Arab history since the late 18th century, Arabic has also acquired a uniquely contested position in modern culture, defended and extolled by its native speakers and writers, belittled, attacked or ignored by foreigners for whom it has represented a last defended bastion of Arabism and Islam.

During the 130 years of French colonialism in Algeria, for example, Arabic was effectively proscribed as a quotidian language: to a lesser degree, the same was roughly true in Tunisia

---

11 Ibid., p. 425.

and Morocco, in which an uneasy bilingualism arose because the French language was politically imposed on the native Arabs.[12]

Silence as an Effect of Violence

Silencing is not always clearly acted out as enforcement on an individual by the colonizers. Sometimes it can result from the colonized experiencing or witnessing the crimes committed against them. Literary critics Al-Naqqash and Abu Shawer confirm that the years following the 1948 Nakba (known also as "the Catastrophe") shocked Palestinian writers especially into stunned bewilderment, driving many into silence for a few years.[13] Since political oppression and subsequent bewilderments continued, the condition of being driven into silence also persisted. This is evident in an interview the poet Mahmoud Darwish gave during the Israeli military siege of Beirut in 1982, where he was living for a few years after being forced into exile. In that interview, which Darwish includes in *Memory for Forgetfulness*, an American journalist asks:

—What are you writing now, poet?
—I am writing my silence.[14] [Darwish replies]

In *Out of Place*, Said points his readers in the direction of another experience that instigates linguistic alienation and necessitates falling silent: being in exile; an experience that millions have undergone today. Said recalls how Arabic was to vanish for many years from his education and life in the United States as it did from the life of other Arabic speakers he encountered. He describes a meeting with a family friend from Egypt after he arrives in the US. Upon seeing this person, Said rushes to speak to him in Arabic in an attempt to establish a sense

---

12 Edward W. Said, "Goodbye to Mahfouz," *The London Review of Books*, vol. 10, no. 22 (1988), https://www.lrb.co.uk/the-paper/v10/n22/edward-said/goodbye-to-mahfouz, accessed April 8, 2022.
13 Khaled Mattawa, "When the Poet Is a Stranger: Poetry and Agency in Tagore, Walcott, and Darwish," PhD Diss. Department of English, Duke University, 2009, https://hdl.handle.net/10161/1289, accessed September 25, 2022.
14 Mahmoud Darwish, quoted from Ibid., p. 282.

of familiarity and intimacy between the two of them. However, the friend stops him immediately, saying something to the effect that he had left that language behind.

Encouragement to bury their own language in silence is commonplace among émigrés, exiles, and refugees. Once they arrive in a new place, they are often expected to abandon their own language and speak the one in use by the dominant group in that place.

The abandonment of one's language is at the core of the institutional assimilation and integration strategies implemented by many governments and their institutions to deal with émigrés, to "rid" them of their histories, cultures, and languages. And whenever the latter do not comply with these strategies, they could be denied full recognition, they may be denied equal status as members of society, and then they may be blamed for their own exclusion. Among other reasons, this is put down to their, the émigrés, insistence on polyphony as a possible means of living together.

In his essay "From Silence to Sound and Back Again," Said elaborates on the émigré's experience of linguist coercion and punishment, pointing out that:

> [This is] the case of someone already invisible and unable to speak at all for political reasons, someone who has been silenced because what he or she might represent is a scandal that undermines existing institutions.
> There is above all the scandal of a different language, then a different race and identity, a different history and tradition: what this results in is either the suppression of difference into complete invisibility and silence, or its transformation into acceptable, but diametrically opposite, identity.[15]

Yet, at the same time, silence does not have a single function and a single meaning. The same way that silence encompasses many muted knowledges and languages between its folds, it also encompasses many experiences. Other instances show that resorting to silence under colonial rule or in exile, may stem from a conscious decision not to engage in dialogue with the colonizer or the powerful elite. By refusing

---

15 Said, *Reflections on Exile and Other Essays*, p. 482.

to speak; by retreating into silence, one may resist becoming a partner in the discourse of the powerful or assuming its logic and its linguistic methods and tools. The silence of Palestinian political prisoners in front of Israeli interrogators, for example, is ultimately the only means available for them to resist their oppressors. Silence in the mouths of these prisoners becomes a tool of resistance rather than an effect of oppression. In effect resorting to silence as a means of self-defense rather than treating it as a foe, is the advice given to anyone engaged in the struggle for freedom should they get arrested.

  In so doing, these prisoners and revolutionaries are no different from the writers who assume silence as, similarly, they attempt to express themselves freely in the form of literature. James Joyce has Stephen Dedalus announce in the novel *A Portrait of the Artist as a Young Man*: "I will try to express myself in some mode of life or art as freely as I can and as wholly as I can, using for my defence the only arms I allow myself to use—silence, exile, cunning."[16]
  Drawing on Dedalus' announcement, Said reaffirms:

> [B]etter that silence than the hijacking of language which is the dominant note of our age. [...] There are then the alternatives either of silence, exile, cunning, withdrawal into self and solitude, or more to my liking, though deeply flawed and perhaps too marginalized, that of the intellectual whose vocation it is to speak the truth to power, to reject the official discourse of orthodoxy and authority, [...] trying to articulate the silent testimony of lived suffering and stifled experience. There is no sound, no articulation that is adequate to what injustice and power inflict on the poor, the disadvantaged, and the disinherited. But there are approximations to it, not representations of it, which have the effect of punctuating discourse with disenchantment and demystifications. To have that opportunity is at least something.[17]

The silence that precedes the approximation that Said recounts here, is an echo of Darwish's deliberation on the silence that precedes poetry; a silence that frees language from only performing the role of pure

---

16 Ibid., p. 486.
17 Ibid.

expression, which is inherent to the experience of the disadvantaged. And both, Said and Darwish echo by taking this stance what Césaire expressed in several of his writings, initially in his long poem *Return to My Native Land*:

> an old silence broken by tepid pustules,
> the dreadful zero of our reason for living.[18]

While Césaire recognizes silence as inescapable in the life of the colonized, in *Discourse on Colonialism* he tries so establish the idea that a writer's role is not so much to reveal the silence of the colonized as much as to shatter the descriptions of it by the colonizers. Only this will allow a new language to emerge; a poetic space that is to be filled by peoples who can speak for themselves at last. For instance, Césaire reveals in his essay "Poetry and Cognition" that it is through poetry, nothing else, with its revolutionary nature, that people can finally speak for themselves. In this proposal, Césaire embraces poetry as a method for achieving insight and of obtaining the kind of language and knowledge that is needed to move forward, arguing that "Poetic knowledge is born in the great silence of scientific knowledge."[19] But what about the nature of the writer of such poetry; the nature of the writer of a literary text; a potential betrayer of their language?

> The master of laughter?
> The master of fearful silence?
> The master of hope and despair?
> The master of idleness? Master of dance?
> It is I![20]

18 Aimé Césaire, *Return to my Native Land*. New York: Archipelago Books, 2013/1939, p. 10.
19 Aimé Césaire (1945), quoted from Robin D. G. Kelly, "Introduction: A Poetics of Anticolonialism," in *Discourse on Colonialism*, pp. 7–28, here p. 17.
20 Césaire, *Return to my Native Land*.

collapse

a thunderstorm

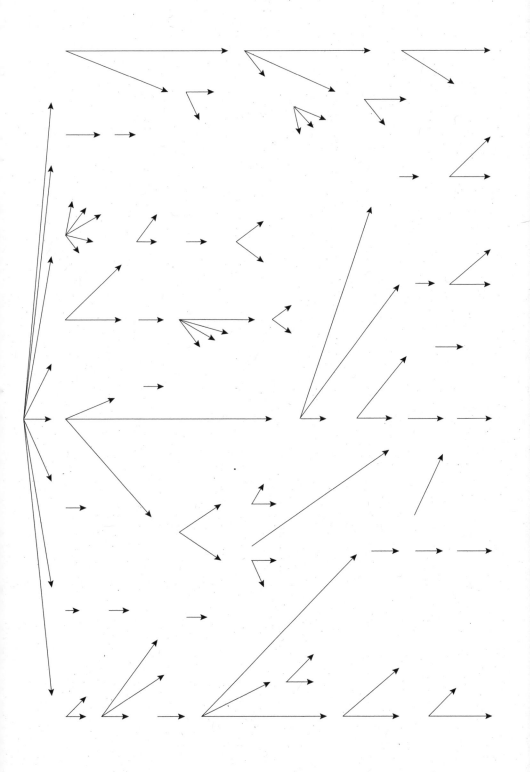

In Search of New Institutional Practice:
A Navigational Conversation

Navigating the Anthropocene

Bernd Scherer: Let me start this conversation with a short description of the situation we are in, why we need new forms of institution, why we need new practices. In my view, we are confronted with two existential crises. First, we are heading towards the collapse of the planetary system and, second, the disintegration of societies, the implosion of liberal democracies. Let me say a few words about the ecological crisis. We at Haus der Kulturen der Welt (HKW) have been addressing this radical transformation for about ten years in the *Anthropocene Project*. The core idea of the Anthropocene thesis is that humans do not merely intervene in nature, but severely destabilize the planet and the climate. This is caused primarily by the extraction of the planet's fossil resources. What took the planet millions of years to produce, humans extract in a very short time, propelled by technological developments and a kind of turbo-capitalism. Scientists speak of the Great Acceleration: most of the major parameters of the Earth system, such as the carbon cycle or the nitrogen cycle, are radically transformed, there is a radical loss of biodiversity, etcetera. In this situation, scientific knowledge no longer describes reality, but—by being translated into technologies and ever faster rhythms—produces new realities. A technological cycle today only lasts about ten years. Consequently, the conception of knowledge production within classical disciplines is dysfunctional. We no longer observe the world from a distant vantage point but navigate within worlds, with knowledge production and world production intertwined by permanent feedback loops. For example, the geologists working on the Anthropocene thesis had to start from the realization that they are not only looking at a new Earth epoch, but that they themselves are some of the major actors in it, because their expertise is used to find fossil energies worldwide. They are no longer scientists observing from above, but actors situated within and affected by these processes. We no longer need a representational knowledge that tells us what the world is, but an interactive knowledge that allows us to navigate within the world. In other words, we must move from fact-based knowledge towards procedural knowledge. Procedures are not fixed, they cannot be simply applied, they must be developed based on concrete issues.

At the same time, we observe a profound inequality between those who profit from and those who are the objects and victims of these developments. We encounter new forms of colonial exploitation: in mines in Africa, in the context of soil desertification processes, and so on. We must therefore change perspective from the eyes of the experts who operate in existing frameworks to the eyes of the people affected by the crisis. They are the experts of their lives and their living environments. That has three major implications for knowledge production: first, we need an activist knowledge, developed by the people who are affected. Secondly, since knowledge cannot simply be applied, we need an aesthetic sensitivity, a knowledge where the senses make sense. And third, knowledge must be formed out of the different perspectives, which is a poetic process. In working on a theme and issue together with the various actors involved, a community arises. World construction, knowledge processes, and community building are different aspects of the same process. Therefore, I think it is very important to not just look at the global or planetary dimensions, but to concentrate on microcosms and analyze how the planetary issues unfold in them.

Maria Hlavajova: Your proposition of "navigation" and knowledge production as a creative process is key to understanding the role of artistic and intellectual practices in the current conjuncture, in my view. While you referred mainly to science, I think the same applies to artistic practices. Much like scientists, the artists of the historical avant-gardes thought of themselves as being outside of or even above society. It is as if the artists "fell" *into* society from a place above it, outsiders that thus lost an ability to give an overview, if you will. That position has become unattainable under current circumstances. But being part of society means being able to connect to the society from below, as it were, with which comes a sense of solidarity and accompliceship. I think of all this as *relational*, similar in movement to what you described as a shift from the representational to the interactive. The consequences for knowledge production in, with, and through art pivot around this need to shift from representation to relation.

Further to your introductory notes, in which you referred to two separate crises: I wonder whether we should think of these two crises, the ecological and the social one, as being one gigantic and complex condition that we find ourselves in.

Navigating Institutions, States, and Colonialism

Adania Shibli: I would say that artistic practice itself navigates. So, navigation is essential to the artistic process, especially when it comes to writing. A writer doesn't try to replace anything but is sensitive to that which is almost there but doesn't have its place yet, trying to find it in language.

It is very difficult, you need to be constantly alert and work with brokenness, incompleteness, and a general fogginess. So power processes cannot come together and replace each other, they must continue in an almost parallel way, allowing new knowledges to constantly form and reform. And the issue of language is key here.

I was thinking about institutions as such and what type of institutions we can think of that are situated somehow outside the state apparatus. I am not against institutions per se, sometimes you must deal with water pipes and electricity and the institutions that deal with that infrastructure.

In the context of Palestine, many of its governing institutions have been preceded by the Israeli authorities. Then you have interventions by the United Nations and institutions that try to manage life under occupation. Third, there are the NGOs, which are a different kind of institution that try to work in parallel with the state institutions.

Here is an example from my teaching at Birzeit University. I have often thought about the panopticon as a structure. The minute there is an Israeli soldier present, there are these panoptic powers that continue to produce surveillance. If you take the Israeli soldier out and put a Palestinian fighter or a revolutionary in the soldier's place, the structure will continue to create surveillance. So, we were discussing an excerpt of the text on the panopticon during class. The students are encouraged to take a text and do whatever they want with it, wherever they want, and they decided to read and discuss it in Hebron/Al-Khalil. The student who had decided to read this text, named Jihad, had been in prison for seven years for political reasons. Other students arranged everything related to the trip, including the buses. We prepared to go to Hebron, and the university says: if somebody gets hurt, shot, or whatever, it's their responsibility. Here, the institution is saying that the minute you pass its walls—because Birzeit is a gated university—personal security is your own responsibility. Then, we arrive in Hebron, in Al-Shuhada Street, the Martyr's Street. This a very heavily surveilled area, with a lot of military and settlers. We all get off the buses, 170 students, all Palestinians, and Jihad wants to go to this big tower, where there are five or six soldiers, and use it as a real-life example to explain what a panopticon is. So, we have this situation: there's a tower and 170 students are gathering around it, almost besieging it. I am in a state of extreme anxiety, because the soldiers are up there, and they might shoot at us at any moment. We all feel this tension, but somehow everybody bursts into laughter, which is kind of a companion reaction to tension. Jihad started using the soldiers and that tower as his example, so they all became figures in his analysis of the panopticon. And it occurred to me there: we do not always have to submit to what has been defined as the only function of a structure. Instead, we can allow the structure to receive different, completely unrelated meanings. In this case, it becomes a theatrical object with a totally different function. We can see the soldiers; the glass was not too dark, as they want to be seen. When they saw us approaching, they stood up. They know, of course, that we cannot do anything, that we are just walking towards the tower, which is very high and made of cement, so there is no chance of us doing anything to them nor to it, we cannot shake it as a structure. And then after some time, the soldiers became bored: "What can you do with these young people who are holding papers and laughing and circulating us?" I kept this example in mind when thinking about institutions, how they can gain new kinds of meaning, how we can unearth a language that has almost been forgotten as a result of a constant use of one certain language, but we can still retrieve that which has been almost completely forgotten by constantly struggling with it.

Eyal Weizman: I think that when you take navigation as a form of knowledge production, or as a form of collaboration, or as a form of political alliance, then you go across and through the borders of the state rather than operate within it and its institutions.

Let me give an example from one of Forensic Architecture's latest commissions, a request for recognition from the Herero people in Namibia that sought reparations for the German genocide of 1904 to 1908, and indeed for the restitution of their lands. In our conversations we learnt how they were speaking about the loss of a world. I thought about how the world produced there was initially created by the complete destruction of the lifeworld experienced by these people. We were sent several photographs taken before and after the genocide. Many taken before showed Herero villages or German colonial settlements within this sort of pristine West African landscape on the Atlantic Coast, complete with all the tropes of landscape photography. But we had an enormous amount of trouble finding out where these photos were taken. The entire landscape has been transformed. And when we were slowly able to locate them, by analyzing things such as rock formations, we discovered a few things. First, Indigenous villages and the German colonial settlements were located right next to each other. The Germans annihilated and murdered their neighbors. Second, the landscape that we were seeing behind those villages has been completely transformed, the kind of trees, grasses, and the kind of bushes, are completely different. The entire environment in which those photographs were taken does not exist anymore. What does that mean in terms of restitution, in terms of a return? Much like the Palestinians, the Herero are using one of the main principles of decolonization: return. Return of their lands and return to their lands. But a return to what? The environment has not been built over, it is still more or less open landscape. But the plants and the environment have been transformed. You start seeing a relation between two things: a relation between an act of genocide that is prescribed in time—over a few years, starting in 1904—which unleash a slow and gradual process of environmental transformation. What's the relation between them? When you are asking that question starting from a single photograph, you shift from the figures in the image to the ground. It is no longer the object you see, but the landscape in which it is embedded that becomes important. To start reading that one photograph, you need to reconstruct or rebuild the world of which it was a part. You need to start working with botanists, and there is a research institution for classifying the distribution of plants and water at the University of Namibia. But you also need to understand what the weather or the climate was like around the turn of the twentieth century. Meteorological studies were few and far apart as were weather stations at the time, so the information only exists in the inherited intergenerational collective recollection of people, as well as in these photographs. So, our analysis of these photographs will involve meteorologists and botanists from different institutions and places. And this sort of collective memory, embedded in the oral tradition of the people, shows that they have not only been displaced from the environment but that the environment has also been displaced from them. It is a very interesting relation, and I think those connected processes are somehow held together in those photographs.

Navigation means several things here: starting from one point, say a photograph from the turn of the century, moving backwards and forwards in time; moving across disciplines, creating alliances that would allow you to understand what it is that you see, led by Herero groups seeking to effectively create political change. Not only historical recognition as an act of acknowledgement, but effectively as a certain transformation or continuation of a never-fulfilled and never-completed act of decolonization. So, you have a navigation that is both in space and time. You need to move to different spaces, you need to see where the rain line is shifting, how the environment is being transformed; you need to think of this photograph on the scale of the planet, and you need to create a navigation or relation between a multiplicity of institutions. So art and cultural institutions such as HKW are essential, not only in order to display things after the work is done, but also in facilitating or being part of that kind of constellation of practices. That said, the state really doesn't feature there. In Namibia, the state is really part of the problem. To a certain extent, it is a continuation of colonial history. That kind of frame must be broken across by a sort of navigational and relational attitude.

Bottom-up Practices and the Question of Funding

Adania Shibli: I think the skepticism about working with institutions stems from past experiences and from the shifts that are being witnessed. In the case of Palestine, for instance, in the last twenty years, cultural institutions were heavily associated with the post-Oslo negotiation process. Before that, the situation was always shifting, and structures were constantly under attack by the policies of the Israeli occupation. When and if any such institutions existed, they needed to regularly transform, using the methods of guerilla warfare: hiding, trying to work behind the scenes, to be invisible, to find different meeting points. So, it was a totally different experience from the type of institution introduced later, which is a recognizable structure that needs funding to function, sometimes a program, all the planning, engagement from and with certain parts of society. Take for example the Khalil Sakakini Cultural Center. It was created in the mid-1990s with the support of the Palestinian Ministry of Culture, and it was the first almost non-governmental cultural institution in Palestine, named after Sakakini, who was a major Palestinian thinker and educator. But these new specialized institutions have been monitored and controlled to a very detailed level.

The Palestinian authority itself is funded by the United States and the European Union as well as by the World Bank and other institutions. Around 2002, the Ford Foundation tried to introduce the condition that the institutions and cultural organizations it funded should not be associated with terrorism. And their definition of terrorism is basically that, if your brother has been in prison or you yourself have been in prison under the occupation, or if you resist the occupation, then you are a terrorist. If you are politically engaged, you are rejected. So, there is a power standing there telling you how this institution should work and about its association with resistance. It requires a disconnect with any previous experiences and realities, with funding playing a decisive role. The Palestinian cultural workers refused this condition, and so, in the end, the Ford Foundation channeled the money through another foundation without this demand. But now the EU is implementing this same condition and specifically targeting people who are associated with the left, such as Marxists. This excludes most of the people working in these cultural institutions; only if you have no role in society and its concerns and struggles can you get this funding.

Take for example the case of the Palestinian National Theatre in Jerusalem, al-Hakawati, where the Israeli authorities were able to control its work and prevent its funding. It was created in the 1980s in an old cinema by a group of people working in theater. Building this space required so many volunteers, because there was no funding. Everybody worked, everybody came and contributed their knowledge. But with the Israeli authorities controlling Jerusalem, even more so in the aftermath of the Oslo Accords, it was not possible to maintain it as a cultural institution, and changes were forced upon it. They appointed a new director who used to run a youth club supported by the Israeli municipality of Jerusalem. And now the place is completely dead. It is no longer doing anything; it gets shut down, sometimes even because of dance activities, and the Israeli police monitor everything going on there. So, what do you do in this situation? Here, it is not a question of changing the institution. Institutions, especially cultural institutions, are in a situation of occupation, are subject to the same death sentence given to Palestinian culture and Palestinian presence. Al-Hakawati went from this very important space for creating and debating art and cultural life, into this miserable dead zone. Should it exist or shouldn't it? Should we seal its assured death?

Gigi Argyropoulou: Yes, the question of persistence and continuity in relation to institutions and/or instituent forms is very interesting. How does instituting as a practice operate within different cultural landscapes? In Greece during the years of crisis and while society was mobilized, many bottom-up institutions appeared, testing self-practices of survival. These practices didn't stem from a desire for experimentation but from the necessity of reimagining and practicing instituent social forms in that moment. A series of collective, bottom-up, in many cases DIY, social structures and institutions appeared, while established structures and traditional ways of doing were falling apart. Medical clinics, exchange networks, farmers without middlemen, collective food kitchens, refugee accommodation, cultural spaces, and so on—many called it the solidarity movement. In the following years, the crisis intensified, and a series of political events followed; many of these initiatives disappeared due to internal or external challenges, while others persisted by transforming into different structures. Of course, such transformations make us reflect on the questions that movements often face: how might a bottom-up structure interact with sedimented practices, processes, buildings, or even ways of making sense? We often find ourselves in between two positions: the need for institutions, because we do need an infrastructure, and, on the other hand, these fleeting transformative moments of doing together that resist becoming a sustainable structure. Maybe that's why I would use the word continuity rather than sustainability, as continuity for me implies a way of seeing things that aren't always directly related. It can thus embrace disappearance, falling apart, things breaking down, and yet also the possibility of reoccurrence again elsewhere. This elsewhere is not unrelated to what happened before, it is a continuity, a sharing of moments, and a sense of history.

Thinking about the two crises, a personal anecdote comes to mind: in my grandparents' village in Corfu where I usually spend the summers, there is this woman who is an organic farmer, having learned farming by herself through practice. I went to visit her land once, and I was surprised about how intertwined and wild her planting was; the tomato plants were not separated from the eggplants, nor were the cucumbers and peach trees. She explained to me that certain plants support each other in growing without intervention. What might look like a wild mess is actually a complex ecology called permaculture. Of course, this relates to how we treat the planet, but it also might echo how we perhaps understand social ecology and continuity as a way of seeing that recognizes constellations, dependencies, alliances, lines of support.

Radical Publics and the Question of Fascism

Maria Hlavajova: Let me return to the notion of the state, of state institutions versus public institutions versus institutions of the commons. I think that there needs to be some sort of nuancing, because different institutions move in different ways. Doesn't all this come back to the notion of navigation again? Just as knowledge creation is a poetic practice of navigation, I think the institutions navigate in a similar way between these policies and relationalities and the politics of everyday existence within certain infrastructures. For example, it is a given that we exist and operate within nation-states. Navigation is something that could also help us to think through how to relate to this very condition. I often think about BAK (basis voor actuele kunst) as an interlocutor, if you will, in a variety of power differentials within society. I then think about a multidirectional interlocuting, including between care and power—I am aware of the wide brushstrokes of the big claims I'm making—but I find it interesting to think of this practice as a form of negotiating an interstitial space for artistic practices that emerge from social movements on the one hand and state apparatuses on the other. Given the reality within which we operate, we try to accommodate a shift from being "against" the powers that be to being or existing "in spite of" them. Necessarily, it is a "situated," "embodied," and "embedded" practice; I think this is where the discussion about "the" institution in generic terms needs more nuance, taking the concrete conditions within our respective locales into careful consideration.

Crucially, there is the notion of publics. When we talk about bottom-up instituting at BAK, we talk about a variety of navigations through reality as we know it. One of the conundrums here is the constant operation within the framework of "us" versus "them" that is our daily reality. The notion of "radical publics" that has been so important for our work at BAK in "instituting otherwise"—as well as the processes of "extituting"—helps us to understand the communities who place claims or demands on the institution. The relation formed through such a placing of claims is different from the legacy of institutional critique. Radical publics often consider cultural institutions as sites of material and symbolic resources that can be tactically deployed within a variety of struggles. I see extraordinary potential here to reposition art and cultural institutions, with real social, political, and ecological consequences. But claims might also be placed by movements one does not identify with politically, too. What about when those publics that gather around fascist ideas place demands on the institutions? What are the ways of dealing with today's reality and the fascist ideologies and practices of life that have been catapulted into the mainstream?

Eyal Weizman: I am really puzzled by the changing contours and matrix of antifascist thinking. In the reframing of the liberal, postwar arts and cultural institution, antifacism was like "the mandate." It was the brief of the self-proclaimed "international community," also made up of institutions, bound up together in a kind of antifascist struggle. Now, I observe that the word antifascism starts to mean more and more things. In a way, that puts pressure on it; it is instrumentalized to a degree that it starts losing its meaning. One obvious example is the war in Ukraine, dubbed in propaganda concocted by Russia as an antifascist, anti-Nazi war. But fighting this sometimes hampers any critical attitude towards those elements of Ukrainian society that do harbor fascist feelings. We are so uncritical about what is happening there.

Secondly, antiracism, as a big part of the antifascist movement, is currently completely losing its meaning in Germany. Think about the debates around documenta and how, in the name of fighting antisemitism, a certain racist ideology and practice is being promoted. How is this possible? Germany is one of a small handful of countries worldwide where Jews are being continuously killed and attempts are made on their lives for simply being Jews. This is something that needs to be addressed, and the Jewish community itself needs to discuss the issue of its security and how it fits in Germany. To exclude the victim organizations from a debate is not right. But the minute that the debate is about Palestine, they demand the exclusion of Palestinians from the debate; that is equally wrong.

The way in which the discussion is organized and framed puts pressure on what antiracism and antifascism are. If antifascism and antiracism operate as a metalevel to what a cultural institution in a post-Second World War order is, and if there is pressure on antifascism and antiracism, then we need to engage what is happening with this meta-concept, because we are seeing symptoms, a thunderstorm of symptoms, based on the collapse of that order. The categories in which we are framing our cultural and institutional politics are crumbling.

Gigi Argyropoulou: Antonio Gramsci discussed hegemony in relation to common sense as that which is established through a form of accepted thinking, while Cornelius Castoriadis talked about the social imaginary, which effects every form of social life. Well, that might be a long discussion, but we now see with the war in Ukraine the same thing we have seen with the COVID crisis and other instances: a clear polarization, an attempt at governance that consists of simplistic positions. I think the question is: in what ways can institutions start to challenge this simplistic common sense and allow spaces for critical reflection? But that requires a certain form of autonomy.

Towards Alternative Practices: Opacity and Fictioning

Adania Shibli: Let me pick up what Maria proposed in terms of the nation-state and dichotomies. I think it is a central question for those institutions not locked into this type of structure. Most of the work of institutions happens within the frame of the state; how can other possibilities emerge that are not bound by that? Maybe navigation is indeed the central term here, because it allows for this zone that is outside of categorization. Also, it goes back to what Khalil al-Sakakini himself was doing. I mentioned earlier that he was an important thinker. He worked in the field of education under the Ottoman Office of Education and later under the British administration, trying to establish a different set of relations within the education system, including by creating a free school. In 1919, he posted a little advert inviting students to participate in a "joint exploration." For me, this confirms that he takes language not as an instrument to articulate, but almost, as he says it, as a domain within which to function and to create your own ethics, where education means growing and taking care of, while still nourishing differences. What does this mean with regards to difference and how you function within these differences? The whole of modernity is somehow built on this tension between opposites and dualities. But in the tradition of Sakakini and how he related to language, there is another route.

Take the word in Arabic for difference, *ikhtilaf*; the roots—in Arabic you always go back to the three-letter root of a word—is *kh.l.f*, meaning to leave traces behind, or coming after. Whereas *khallafa* refers to procreation. So, the possibilities of the word "difference" are about when you give a life and when you leave traces. I mention this, like in the example of the students, to bring us somewhere else, like a storm that turns things around, to free something from the specific reality that one is constantly struggling with. Like a possibility that has been covered underneath the rubble of so many other practices, and you labor to salvage it from under the rubble, alive.

Considering this and coming back to the nation-state, I am wondering, and I think many Palestinians are wondering—since we have been the victims of a state project over the past seven or eight decades—do we want to adapt to this exact model? We experienced what the nation-state is capable of when you are not part of it, when this kind of state unleashes its wrath based on differences. Could we go in a totally different direction? We certainly cannot just accept it as the only possible way of functioning.

Maria Hlavajova: In light of the current political situation, I would argue for reviving the thoughts and practices of the Non-Aligned Movement, updated for the needs of our present, and thus extending its potentials beyond the nation-state. Non-alignment in the twentieth century is often understood as a position of political "neutrality," when instead it was prompted to existence by a need to collectively seek radical possibilities outside of the competition of two imperialist powers vying for dominance. The way I studied it alongside the "Former West" project, at its core, was a radical discourse around peace, justice, and equality. I wonder whether this is a way to capture the possibility of this moment. At present, I'm also reminded continuously about my coming of age in totalitarian Czechoslovakia under what was effectively Russian occupation. There is a key text from 1978 called "The Parallel 'Polis'" by Václav Benda, spokesperson for Charter 77. He formulates the idea of building a parallel polis as a way of utterly committing to a publicness of another sort than what was available under the regime of the day. It reminds me of the need to re-calibrate our practice from transparency and openness—all these great modernist ideas—into, perhaps, opacity or semi-opacity and to revisit the possibility of creating sanctuaries to conduct certain diffi-cult discussions. Art can facilitate such spaces and encourage discus-sion around what might appear politically "unspeakable" currently—think indeed of some of the reckonings with Germany's colonial past at documenta or, say, the divisive issue of the boycott of all cultural practitioners from Russia and Belarus due to the war in Ukraine. Could this belong to the role of art institutions in our times? To close the door now and then, if you will, stop broadcasting everything to everywhere in the world, creating instead a space for in-depth debates of those subjects that are impossible to discuss out in the open?

Gigi Argyropoulou: Can the institution today ever become a space of refuge and close all its doors, considering neoliberal pressure? Insti-tuting certainly operates through both visibility and invisibility; that which becomes visible in a public moment comes about through in-visible moments that made it possible. But is this possible in institu-tions today? How do we value both the visible and the invisible?

Maria Hlavajova: I think the institution is much more than the sum of its public events. The metaphor of "mushrooming" is what I some-times use in regard to BAK. Mushrooms could not come to fruition without the feeding structure of hyphae under the ground. I like to think of BAK mostly as the mycelium-like infrastructure, and the mushrooms—the events—as an intermittent surfacing of the nourish-ing processes. The ultimate purpose of the fruiting body being to seed back into the fungi underground...

There is also the notion of fictioning as a method to allow certain conversations to unfold which might be otherwise impossible. I think of this as a practice of politico-aesthetic experimentation aided by fic-tion so as to maintain the capacity to live political life in common. The question is: what can we do openly that does not endanger anybody but allows us, despite this horrible situation at hand, to do something?

Eyal Weizman: I think fictioning is necessary on so many levels. The art space needs room for very different kinds of experimentation.

Therefore, I would call it aesthetic practice, poetic practice, or collective practice, and many other things. I refuse the distinction that fictionalization rests on a certain dichotomy between certainty and speculation, separating a domain of fact from a domain of imagination. In fact, bridging those gaps between imagination, aesthetics, and facts is a necessary practice. In that sense, what is not fictional? There are so many ways of engaging our life, our possibilities, and our future that also combine and cut across that fiction–nonfiction divide. In many of the works of art that I love, there is a grain of documentary, recorded information that is later worked in through a multiplicity of imaginary and aesthetic practices. The fiction–nonfiction divide puts practices into a silo, much like the silos of institutions, nation-states, or disciplines. Weaving between facts, navigating in a potentially imaginary, aesthetic, or poetic way, is essential. Once you understand that truth is a value, a social and political value we give to facts, you start having many transversal kinds of relations in which practitioners of documentary forms and artists together with scientists, etcetera, could come together to build a community of practice that is engaged with a description of the world that is not representational but procedural. It is an act of intervention. The debate around particular facts and the way that they are produced is politically and aesthetically productive. It is not simply an issue of representation that comes after the fact, but part of the production itself.

Maria Hlavajova: Fiction is not the opposite of truth or facts.

Eyal Weizman: Or nonfiction, right?

Maria Hlavajova: This makes me think of Ursula K. Le Guin's response to a statement made about the Trump administration, its "alternative facts," and their similarity to science fiction. In response, Le Guin stressed that a fact has no alternative. "To pretend the sun can rise in the west is a fiction," she said, but "to claim that it does so as fact (or 'alternative fact') is a lie."

In complex times like ours—think the difficult conversations to be had in a classroom, for example bringing together the perspectives of my Ukrainian and Russian students—fictioning can allow another kind of time–space entity to exist; we can rehearse another possibility, another relationality, another world.

Adania Shibli: Speaking of opacity as a different tool reminds me of other practices such as cunning. We can see this in the encounter between Bertolt Brecht and the House Un-American Activities Committee that subjected him and his "communist tendencies" to an investigation. They quoted a poem he wrote that they described as revolutionary. In a very insistent and accusative tone, they asked him "Did you write that, Mr. Brecht?," thinking this poem would implicate him by revealing these communist tendencies. Turning it into something completely different—namely a linguistic interrogation, a place that matters for him—he replied, "No. I wrote a German poem, but that is very different from this." This goes back to what I said about not being driven into conversations that are hijacked and violent in their hijacking. The accusation that Sakakini was a Hitler sympathizer, for example, is almost violent, not violent as such but it is almost cultural violence. He decried chauvinism and hid a Jewish American at his home against an Ottoman decree during the Second World War, which put him at risk of being hanged. So, there is a violent fictioning within that too. We should maybe look at these acts and all their relations to violence and how we can face this violence without being dragged into its logic. We may go down a different path, take the conversation somewhere else when we feel almost defeated, violated. I also wonder about the violence that is there in institutions and how these institutions can address such violence. It is something that we didn't really talk about in this conversation, but it is there. Maybe it is subtler than that, maybe it is more taken for granted, but there is this aspect of violence there.

Bernd Scherer: Thank you all for this lively conversation. In conclusion, I would like to briefly raise the question of the future role of the institution. There is one interesting point in Eyal's essay that also reflects, to some extent, the practice of HKW and also Maria's and Gigi's practice. We develop projects with people who need our solidarity. Eyal described it in a very nice way: we as an institution don't do projects, the institutional part of our practice consists of weaving projects together. And weaving projects together is building up reality on the one side, but also building up social communities in doing so. So, it's a community-building process, a reality-building process, and a knowledge-building process. I would say, instead of institutions having authority and being legitimized by being institutions, this practice of weaving knowledges, communities, and realities together could be a very interesting perspective on institutional work in the future. And to add a final point: could these different institutional practices also be interwoven with each other? During this conversation, it became very clear that we all share common attitudes, common positions, and common practices which, hopefully, could be connected to each other in some way or the other.

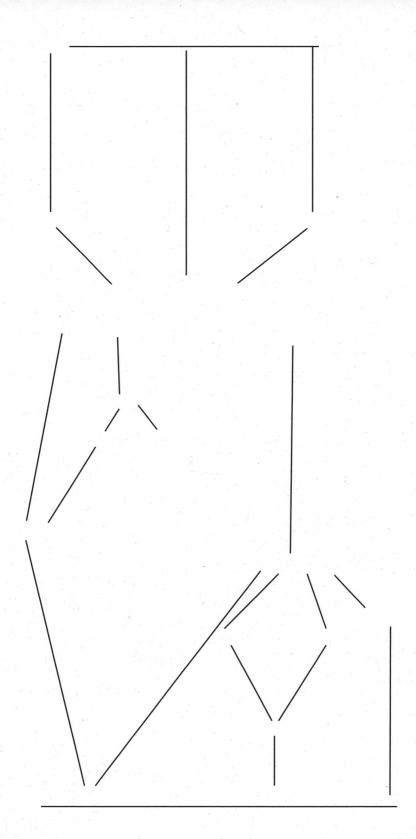

Open Verification

If somebody told me a decade ago that I would be running a forensic institute, I would have run for my life. I found the very idea of forensics rather abhorrent. Schooled in critical studies and coming from the field of leftist activism, I felt more at home positioning myself against the authority of established truths. Forensics relies on technical expertise and involves the presentation of opinion within normative frameworks and according to legal protocols. It smacked of institutional authority. It is, after all, one of the fundamental arts of the state, the privilege of its agencies: the police, the secret services, or the military.

Today, I find myself directing Forensic Architecture (and its new sister agency FORENSIS in Berlin) whose members include architects, filmmakers, artists, coders, lawyers, and journalists. This shift is due to changes within the political and technological texture of our present. But what enabled the shift was primarily a certain conceptual inversion. Key to the reorientation of my thought practice is the notion of *counter-forensics*—a turning around of the forensic gaze in order to investigate those state agencies that normally practice forensics themselves. Indeed, our agencies are focused primarily on state crime, and we have never, though they tried, knowingly taken a commission from a state agency.

Our work usually involves two kinds of actions: we deconstruct the statements of those in power, show their weaknesses and inconsistencies, bring doubt where official pronouncements make facts appear solidly in favor of those in power, and we also use a multiplicity of evidentiary sources to construct (something of) the narrative of what may have taken place.

That is, we both destroy statements of fact, and we build them. I have written elsewhere about the way in which, as a form of inquiry, the "investigative mode" is distinct from the "critical mode" that we have been accustomed to in the fields of the arts and humanities.

They are distinct, it is true, but the investigative doesn't dismiss criticality. Crucially, investigation involves mediation. The critical approach's tendency of suspicion is essential in exposing the gaps, inconsistencies, biases, lacunae, traces of manipulation, and misrepresentations in the statements of those in power—in highlighting places where habit and naturalized common sense might otherwise compel us to see facts. It is also true that a critical approach can have a constructive function. When we understand how facts are made, where their weaknesses lie, and where the limits of what can be said are, we can better construct and defend ours.

Over the past decade, we have used our methods to undertake more than seventy investigations worldwide—police officers shooting civilians, militaries engaging in indiscriminate urban destruction, illegal incarceration in secret prisons, and environmental destruction by states and corporations among many others.[1]

Counter-forensics is distinct from the forensics that emerged out of the intersection of policing and science in the nineteenth century— it is not as if the people stormed the lab and took it over. This difference is partly due to some structural limitations on the work of those investigating state crime. Primary amongst those limitations is the exclusion of those practicing counter-forensics from the crime scene. They are kept beyond the literal and figurative police tape. The evidentiary basis for counter-forensics must rely upon information which slips through or under this police cordon; something leaks, victims of violence share images or videos and testify publicly or directly to us; border guards or police might leak information intentionally or accidentally through social media. Our evidentiary base thus tends to be partial. We call these partial but crucial bits of data "weak signals."

There is another space we sometimes find ourselves excluded from: the legal forums of states do not always welcome those investigating state crimes. If and when we are admitted, we are confronted with an obvious fact: these forums are never neutral. The protocols of each condition the presentation of evidence in different ways. Some things can be said and others not. We thus seek to offset the problem

---

1   We exposed the connection between a German secret-service agent and
    a racially motivated murder by neo-Nazis; presented findings on drone
    strikes to the UN General Assembly; contributed to the conviction of
    senior members of the Greek neo-Nazi group Golden Dawn; used artificial
    intelligence (AI) to provide evidence of Russia's 2014 invasion of Ukraine
    to the European Court of Human Rights (ECHR); helped to stop the
    perpetrators of illegal forest fires in Indonesia; identified the Turkish
    police officers responsible for the killing of a prominent Kurdish lawyer,
    leading to their prosecution; presented findings on violence against
    migrants at EU borders and thus triggered special sessions of the European
    Parliament; and undertook extensive work for the forthcoming reports of
    the Colombian Truth Commission. See www.forensic-architecture.org.

of forum-specific limitation on speech by migrating our evidence between different forums as we seek to expand the sites of truth-telling—
from the national or international courtroom (when we are able),
truth commissions, citizen's tribunals, community assemblies, parlia-
mentary inquiries, through to the media, the museum, or gallery, let-
ting our evidence speak a different dialect in each. For the latter fo-
rum, I am forever grateful for the structural support we received along
the way from Bernd Scherer, Anselm Franke, and the rest of the team
at Haus der Kulturen der Welt (HKW), Berlin, which facilitated and
supported several of our investigations, both conceptually and physically, staging a number of exhibitions and events including our inau-
gural one, *FORENSIS*, from which the name of our Berlin-based agency is derived. This kind of collaboration demonstrates the principle of
open verification discussed in these pages.

Our casework brought us into close contact with different political events, with developments in media technologies and media environments. Such encounters provided opportunities for reflections
on the social, technological, and political "life" of facts and produced
advances in our thought regarding the relation between technology,
politics, and truth practices.

Anti-Epistemology

A certain reality-denial which presently manifests itself in digital racism, ultra-nationalism, self-victimhood, and conspiracism—more recently called "post-truth"—is not akin to what Hannah Arendt called
"lying in politics." Deception is sometimes necessary. This phenomenon is not manifested as an epistemological argument about the ve-
racity of this or that fact or as a debate about how best to establish or
verify things. It is rather an attempt by some types of regimes to cast
doubt over the very possibility of there being a way to reliably establish facts at all, thus blurring people's perception, with those in power
filling this void with the clarity of ideological proclamation. For such
anti-epistemologies, truth seems simple and given, ready at hand, depending merely on the power of their position. Such acts of reality-denial are not rhetorical add-ons to the brute force of state violence,
rather they are the condition that enables them to continue to happen.
The destruction of evidence tends to complement the destruction of
people and things. If nothing wrong has happened, how is it to stop?

Though often presented as new, this tendency has been around a long time. Those confronting colonialism have always been aware of techniques of perception management, obfuscation of facts regarding violence and dispossession, and the destruction of lifeworlds and the traces of their existence. Colonialism and empire may have had science and technology on their side, but they were, and remain, epistemological wrecking balls that destroy a plenitude of different forms of knowledge and perception. Genocide and ecocide, besides being forms of erasure in themselves, were enabled by the destruction and denial of the evidence of their very occurrence.

The reason that those people in the world that call themselves "WEIRD"—that is, western, educated, industrialized, rich, and democratic—have started speaking of anti-epistemology is because these techniques of conflict management have only recently beached like a carcass onto the shores of mainstream politics.

To some extent, we have ourselves to blame. Mainstream liberal politics sometimes elevates scientific authority over truth, rendering it unquestionable. If this form of politics demands belief in the form of simple allegiance ("don't you believe in science?"), this results in the institutions of science sometimes taking on something of the guise of their theological predecessors—inherently true, beyond reproach, with transcendental qualities. When this epistemic order becomes identifiable within liberal politics, the enemies of the status quo may have a justifiable need to rebel. If the institutions of truth demand belief in the form of simple allegiance, then no doubt what we see is a kind of inchoate mutiny in which opposition will, in some respects, be seen as a rebellion against Rome. Indeed, few of the current crop of anti-epistemologists have been slow to cast themselves in the image of insurgent speakers of truth to power. This leads to questioning the expertise of top research universities, known science laboratories, think tanks, mainstream (or quality) media, and the judiciary.

Even in our field, we gradually started to gain firsthand knowledge of how a well-meaning project that refuses the role of "expert" can drift into this categorization. It is a process by which ideas become a project (through funding), the project becomes an organization (through bureaucracy), the organization starts being seen as an institution (though it is not), and the institution, as institutions do, started gaining/losing, like it or not, institutional authority.

* * *

The obscuring, blurring, and distortion of facts in the field of state crime and human rights requires attacks against networks of truth production and nodes within those networks: the groups, organizations, individuals, or media platforms, that construct facts. When they collaborate, it is the relation between them that is targeted. Knowledge production necessitates relations between different institutions and experts. For anti-epistemologists, it is enough to point at a weak or "contaminating" node—an individual or an organization within a collaborative system of knowledge production (which may or may not have been involved in this or that wrongdoing, error, or mischief in their opinion)—to claim that the whole network can't hold.

A dilemma presents itself in facing such anti-epistemology. If the attack on mainstream established institutional expertise is a quest for the destruction of the old epistemic order, a tempting response might be to buttress the familiar custodians of factual authority—the academy, journalism, public administration, the judiciary, the police, perhaps even the FBI or other intelligence services—that seem to be holding together the "liberal epistemic order." Defending some of the very institutions we dislike in fear of an alternative can be understood as rearguard attrition warfare. Can we rather take the challenge, let them fall, and plunge on?

Yes, but taking this challenge presents another difficulty. Counter-forensics may seem strangely similar to anti-epistemology. Both seem to be aligned against the epistemic authority of state institutions—the same police, judiciary, secret service, government, and military—both seek to expose conspiracies, cover-ups, lies in the heart of power, and both are sensitive to instances in which the legal system has been abused. Even seeking to disable nodes within an epistemic system of knowledge production seems like a classic move of critical theory, deconstruction, and counter-forensics.

However, such similarity, existing as it does, is misleading. There is a crucial difference: the current politics of denial has never provided the basis for the production of an alternative counter-hegemonic knowledge or new models of truth practice.

The aim of counter-forensics is to challenge both the anti-epistemology of the present as well as the more traditional pillars and platforms of truth production. The attempt is to respond to the current skepticism towards expertise not with the relativism of "anything goes" and its unchecked declarations of fact, but with a vital and risky form of truth production, based on wide networks of participatory research practice and the incorporation of aesthetic and scientific sensibilities. The one I will describe is not nested within institutions of authority but cuts through them, wiring them up in ever more complex and strange ways.

Such investigative practice should be rigorous (of course) but also collective; locally grounded, but diffuse. The assumption of counter-forensics is that, if a greater number and a wider diversity of parties is involved in the investigation, we can address the institutional crisis as well as the lack of trust in facts. One of the ways to address the epistemic crisis of the present is by expanding participation in evidence production and dissemination, by socializing the development and deployment of human rights-based evidence through collaboration with frontline communities, thus resisting manifestations of this counterfactual tendency. This will expose investigations to the cannons of anti-epistemology. But this doesn't matter, it is not them that we need to convince.

This practice does not simply demand an opening and a levelling up. Every knowledge-seeking practice relies on forms of specialisms. Participants bring with them unique forms of expertise, situated, embodied, practiced, and learned, that need to be integrated with the whole. We shouldn't flatten out expertise and experience but network and recombine them in different ways. This is a chaotic but much-needed process.

Counter-forensics also seeks to establish new alignments between different sites, styles, and institutions of diverse types and standings. These include the science laboratory, the artist's studio, the university, activist organizations, social groups, and art and cultural spaces. It seeks to create a poly-perspectival assemblage of open epistemic and aesthetic multiplicity. As such, the process of investigation might itself establish a social contract that includes all the participants in this assemblage. Investigations produced in the context of this project will not only be evidence of what has happened, but also of the social relations which made them possible. New investigative practices should not only be thought of as a given set of techniques, but as grounded in (and feeding back into) new modes of social organization and arrangements of labor.

Open Verification

It might be altogether necessary to employ the word "truth" differently. In opposition to the single perspectival, a priori, sometimes transcendent conception of truth embodied by the Latin word *veritas*—which connotes the authority of an expert working within a well-established discipline—a term more suitable for our work (and of the same root) is *verification*. Verification relates to truth not as a noun or as an essence, but as a practice, one that is immanent, contingent, collective, and poly-perspectival.

The term verification belongs to the history and theory of science. It charges empirical observation with the task of confirming or falsifying an abstract proposition, be it a mathematical model, scientific theory, or philosophical conjecture. In the field of counter-forensics, "open verification" engages with new kinds of material—open source and activist produced—employing different methodological processes that open and socialize the production of evidence, integrate scientific with aesthetic sensibilities, and work across and bring together different types of seemingly incompatible institutions and forms of knowledge.

Because it starts from an incident, open verification is grounded in experience, and the perspective it brings to bear is openly partial, embedded, activist, or militant, rather than a "disinterested" or "neutral" view from nowhere. Patiently adding different local, ground-level perspectives to one another allows for an incident to be seen from different points of view. With a greater number of perspectives included, more relations can be established between the actors, perpetrators, victims, and bystanders in a scene.

Open verification integrates a distributed network of practitioners working together with the victims to articulate the logic of the violence inflicted upon them: communities collecting information in videos and testimonies; activists and lawyers who stand with them; technologists and scientists (in areas as diverse as structural engineering, botany, geology, fluid dynamics, and remote sensing) who augment user-produced evidence with their distinct skill set. Thereafter come reporters, publishers, and cultural institutions, with their curators offering forums in which evidence is circulated and framed within broader historical and sometimes theoretical contexts.

Collaborating with art and cultural venues is not only a pragmatic move. Forensics and curatorial practices share a deep concern for knowledge production and display, for the presentation of ideas and issues through the arrangements of evidence, objects, conversations, screenings, or bodies in space.

Open verification can never take trust for granted. While the probity of traditional expert testimony—when presented in the context of a trial or to the general public—lies in the credentials and reputation of scientists or their institutions, the probity of open verification must be in its making. The burden of open verification is to gain trust and remain as open and transparent as possible in the processes by which truth claims are made and facts established. Open verification needs to continuously expose every step by which the work was carried out—its circumstances, the people involved, the materials used, how and where each piece of evidentiary material was found, its modes of authentication, and the means by which different pieces of evidence were brought together and a case was assembled. Doing this allows for the public domain to function in an analogous process to a scientific peer review; that is, the underlying data is examined by others, with the processes able to be replicated and tested. This is the reason that most of the content of our video investigations is a "how-to." The presentation of a case, thus, always needs to record the interaction and interference that were part of its process.

As such, this mode of verification is somewhat analogous to the function of the blockchain in crypto currencies, a mode of security that does not depend on a single solid vault but on the checks and balances of an open community.

Beyond the exposure of our methods and the amount of information woven together, open verification must be persuasive through the force of its narrative, the momentum of its collectivity, and the rhetoric of its presentation in image, video, text, and sound. To make a change, it needs to be mobilized as part of a social-political process, and for this, social alliances need to be built, and cultural institutions must form part of the process.

Open verification often starts from a site or a specific point: a controversy, a local debate, an accident, a detail. From this point of individuation, an investigation follows different threads that lead outwards along complex paths of causality. Disentangling these threads necessitates different forms of knowledge, experience, and expertise.

It is in this way that the systemic conditions of a larger political context reveal themselves in incidents. Examples of this can be found in our series of works on police violence entitled "The Long Duration of the Split Second." Each of these works investigates a different incident of police shootings in the United States of America, the United Kingdom, Greece, Palestine, and Turkey. These shootings are defended under the "split-second argument," where an officer claims the suspect's right to life is suspended because an imminent threat is perceived "in the heat of the moment." This defense relies on the notion of natural instinct. But this instinct is culturally and politically produced and can be traced to a long history of the structural violence of colonization, segregation, and domination that dehumanized the colonized and the enslaved, turning them into legitimate prey.

There is a huge epistemological, temporal, and geographical space to be traversed from the detail of the incident to larger historical contexts. The investigative work moves between the scales of the locally, politically, and culturally entrained to vast geographies and histories. Combining the detail of the incident with wider forms of understanding requires bringing together different forms of knowledge that can also often test each other. To trace evidentiary threads requires labor and care.

Investigative Aesthetics

Collaborating with art and cultural institutions is also an opportunity to rework the notion of aesthetics.

Aesthetics is becoming manifest in areas more traditionally understood as investigative, in fields such as science, journalism, data analytics, critical computing, law, and human rights. Journalists and human rights analysts pore over and construct visual or filmic investigations without necessarily being explicitly aware of the ways their fields have become aesthetically activated. Aesthetics is not an extra dimension but a crucial ingredient that activates different fields and brings them together.

In other ways, "aesthetics" and "investigation" do not fit comfortably, of course. The terms "aesthetics" and "to aestheticize" seem to be anathema to familiar investigative paradigms, because they signal manipulation, emotional or illusionistic trickery, the expression of feelings, and the arts of rhetoric rather than the careful protocols of truth. These are difficult preconceptions to overcome, especially in confronting state authorities. Aesthetic considerations can be read as markers of a lack of earnestness, gravity, and sincerity that might divert the quest of finding things out.

In *Investigative Aesthetics*, a book I have written with media theorist Matthew Fuller—from which these thoughts are derived—we align with those for whom aesthetics is not an act of beautification, but rather one of careful attunement, one of noticing and bringing observations together into an act of construction. Investigative aesthetics—the encounter between "aesthetics" and "investigation"—could be an opportunity to shift and expand both constitutive elements.

Rather than putting aesthetics in a separate place or even in opposition to knowledge production, we proposed ways of aligning them. As the capacity to sense and detect, aesthetics has an obvious evidentiary dimension. It is also essential as the mode and means for narration, performance, and staging, all of which are necessary for making evidence public. And it is evident that, when it is mainly images and videos that need to be examined, image producers—photographers and filmmakers—have a crucial role to play.

Aesthetics involves *sensing*—the capacity to register or to be affected—and sense*making*—the capacity for such sensing to become knowledge of some kind. The former is the result of the receptive action of a sensory organ, material, or system. The latter involves experience and understanding of what is being sensed, a perception and conception, or a worldview. The finding or invention of means to achieve such effects is to "aestheticize." In this expanded meaning, aesthetics includes elements that are not exclusively the property of humans. Animals and plants, just like other material surfaces or indeed computing systems, apprehend their environment—detect, register, and predict. Our insistence in the book that aesthetics is active beyond the human, and that sensing is also prevalent in complex technical assemblages, digital detectors, in ecosystems, and in the multiple relations between them, draws on the fading of the antagonistic division of the sciences and humanities.

There are two other related terms we proposed: *hyper-aesthetics*, a ramified state of aesthetic alertness in which both sensing and sensemaking are intensified. Hyper-aesthetics increases sensation by amplifying the sensitivity of an entity to the environment around it and thus increasing the growth of sensemaking experience and the generation and building of assemblies that synthesize multiple sensations. While all matter can potentially be read as sensors, the reorganization of relations between organic and inorganic sensorial matter, people and computers, can increase nonhierarchical sensorial assemblages and even potentially harvest or "rescue" traces from beneath layers of erasure. Hyper-aesthetics becomes particularly palpable through the incorporation of human sensing within a network of devices that monitor, count, and measure. It is an elaboration of this general condition of aesthetics—its interlinkedness—to the point that it mutates and becomes reflexive. This is the foundation for what we have proposed as an *investigative commons*, or even a common sense (different from its meaning as the naturalized epistemological status quo); commons are not necessarily a site of harmonious sustenance and eternal agreement, of course, but of negotiation and even of struggle.

In this book, Matt and I also proposed the term *hyperaesthesia* to describe a condition in which sensual overload "crashes" sensation, when sensing and making sense part ways, when the senses stop making sense, when information overload short-circuits the logic of reason or the capacity for reflection, sometimes leading to psychic disintegration.

Investigative aesthetics is, in part, a process of collectively assembling accounts from images and media flotsam. It involves tuning into and interpreting weak signals and noticing unintentional evidence registered in visual, audio, or data files or in the material composition of our environment. It also refers to the use of aesthetic sensibilities in assembling cases and in editing material into effective films and videos or installations. In these constructions, each found element is not a piece of evidence in itself, but rather an entry point to find connections with others, one part in a heterogeneous assemblage that allows for navigation across and weaving together disparate elements.

Aesthetics as an extremely careful way of noticing is also an ethical position, because opening one's ability to sense is opening oneself to the experience of pain, in opposition to the danger of developing an anesthesia to political injustice which would in turn remove investigation from the proximate relation to the event that it aims to comprehend and trace. There are constantly aesthetic, political, and ethical choices to be made, for example in determining which incidents should be pursued, how wide to open the investigative angle, or working out which aesthetic impressions can become evidence and for what.

Aesthetic Commons

The practice of open verification is one of the avenues through which to re-entangle artistic and scientific work and bring forth a new aesthetics of facts. Rather than objectivity's "view from nowhere," open verification seeks the meshing of multiple, subjective, located, and situated perspectives. Rather than being confined to the black boxes of institutions of authority, it is based on open processes and new alignments between different sites and institutions of diverse types and standings: the science laboratory, the artist studio, the university, activist organizations, victim groups, national and international legal forums, the media, and cultural institutions. However, such extensive investigative networks can often be based on asymmetrical relations, and they must be constructed in ways that recognize and seek to undo the different degrees of privilege and access.

This collective and diffused mode of truth production is made necessary by a political situation in which conflicts are waged not only over resources but over the interpretation of the real, and identities are formed around the formation and interpretation of facts.

State perpetrators and their anti-epistemologists want to destroy the possibility of a common ground. While for us, inversely, establishing the common ground becomes a political project. With each new investigation, a new community of praxis is woven from the meshing of its divergent viewpoints. In this, open verification becomes a form of construction. In socializing the production and dissemination of evidence, it ultimately establishes an unlikely but fundamental commons in which the production of facts constitutes the foundation of an expanded epistemic community of practice built around a shared perception and understanding of the world.

This epistemological commons is a metapolitical condition which forms the ground on which any struggle can take place. Such a commons needs to be continuously remade and reinforced. This commons might seem analogous to a natural resource such as air or a freshwater; as such, we must protect it when it is polluted by the toxins of dark epistemologists. Yet, unlike water and air, it is neither preexisting nor natural, but a social reality that needs to be continuously remade, reinforced, and fought over—more akin, therefore, to the commons of language. It must not be fenced off but kept with its margins open to new information and ever-newer perspectives, evidence, and inter-pretation. As such, it can only grow and morph with disagreement.

Integrating texts by the author from:
Eyal Weizman, "Open Verification," *e-flux* (June 2019), https://www.e-flux.com/architecture/becoming-digital/248062/open-verification/, accessed September 23, 2022.
Eyal Weizman, *Forensic Architecture: Violence at the Threshold of Detectability*. New York: Zone Books, 2017.
Eyal Weizman and Matthew Fuller, *Investigative Aesthetics: Conflicts and Commons in the Politics of Truth*. London: Verso, 2021.
Eyal Weizman and Thomas Keenan, *Mengele's Skull: The Advent of a Forensic Aesthetics*. Berlin: Sternberg Press, 2012.

access

distance

Dislocating Institutions: Theses/Momentums of (Un)Making Spaces of Culture

What if we were to start by dislocating? By focusing on the nexus of connections that is always present in the here and now and makes movement possible. Dislocating as a method of working inside a certain terrain, engaging with a specific context and yet at the same time fleeing from it, seeking strategies to intervene in sedimented practices while also imagining and practicing an elsewhere. Dislocating as the practice of doing otherwise. Not as the privilege of fantasizing a different here and now, but rather as an ongoing implication in the specificities, the materialities, and the strictures of a specific context that, out of necessity, leads to experimenting with the existing modus operandi and the familiar ways of making things work. Dislocating as the practice of unsettling, relating, shifting, inventing, depending, breaking, locating again and again. An experimenting with what could be operating otherwise that comes about as a way to be present in the here and now, a method of survival. As if making, curating, experimenting, and doing were all complicit together in compiling a fragile method that follows the turns and curves of life—every time we struggle to establish a temporary form, a supportive infrastructure.

In recent decades, the discourse/practice around institutions has identified new paths of institutional remaking, intervention, and critique. Whilst neoliberal calls to order seek to offer specific ways to evaluate and measure the impact and productivity of existing institutions, we have also witnessed multiple artistic and social practices that create new publics and emergent, bottom-up practices of commoning. Cultural institutions that have followed the recent turn in social and political tendencies often attempt to transform themselves into "civic places," into places that seek to bring artists close to communities, spaces in which to build and (re)conceive political fronts and incorporate social movements, sites to create new urban publics. It is evident that old institutions have been forced to readjust in order to survive neoliberal reforms whilst, at the same time, discovering ways to remain relevant and respond to the challenges of today. What might the possibilities be of such transformations within existing protocols, forms, and structures? How might we work with complicit and stubborn institutional formats? Kike España and Gerald Raunig argue that the crisis we have experienced in recent years is a multifaceted one that includes "a crisis of institutions and most of all a crisis of subjectivation," suggesting that "institutional critique just does not suffice, if it is fixated on the institution or even on a mere take-over of the institution," because, as they argue, "providing new content, but keeping the institutional form would not be enough."[1] What, then, might be the instituent artistic and curatorial strategies that can offer new viable institutional forms as well as transformative moments of undercommon publics? What are the figurative forms/strategies that might remain resistant to neoliberal recuperation?

Transforming the institutional form into a strategic machine for social organizing, curating, and artistic practice might be something that many of us repeatedly work towards, however it also remains a practice that is often under-discussed and under-theorized. The Invisible Committee argue that "what we need is not institutions but forms [...] everything that lives is an interaction of forms."[2] And yet we might also need to ask: in what environments do these forms take shape, and what other forms do they make possible? What constellations of being and doing do they create, and what traces do they leave behind? And how are these forms shared and inhabited by others?

This reflection brings together four momentums, that is, four situations in which a practical rethinking of the form and modus operandi of cultural spaces became a reality. In different contexts from the last two decades in Southern Europe, diverse spaces of momentum manifested as cultural occupations that enabled a practical rethinking of processes of instituting as well as issues of visibility, organization, and legitimation. Dislocating in a sense of cultural practices, these four diverse experiments could be considered forms

---

1   Kike España and Gerald Raunig, "Monstrous Complicities," in "Instituting" on the *New Alphabet School* website (August 12, 2021), https://newalphabetschool.hkw.de/monstrous-complicities/, accessed March 11, 2022.

2   The Invisible Committee, *Now*, trans. Robert Hurley. South Pasadena, CA: Semiotext(e), 2017, p. 70.

of cultural critique that came about through the making of a DIY/bottom-up institution—as, a mode of collective instituting. Acknowledging political implications and seeking to think together direct actions and curatorial perspectives, writing from an inside-outside perspective,[3] in and through this text, I seek to sketch a possible field of transformative instituent counterstrategies that rethink the possibilities of cultural practice within a specific milieu. Blurring the limits between making and unsettling, experimenting and taking space, materiality and disappearance, visibility and remaining incomplete, homelessness and the desire for a shared space, this open-ended speculation seeks to discuss the potential of transformative momentums as methods for (un)making and reimagining cultural institutions and publics.

1. Material Dependencies

Fugitive publics do not need to be restored. They need to be conserved, which is to say moved, hidden, restarted with the same joke, the same story, always elsewhere than where the long arm of the creditor seeks them, conserved from restoration, beyond justice, beyond law, in bad country, in bad debt. They are planned when they are least expected, planned when they don't follow the process, planned when they escape policy, evade governance, forget themselves, remember themselves, have no need of being forgiven. They are not wrong though they are not finally communities; they are debtors at distance, bad debtors, forgotten but never forgiven.[4]

---

3   I have been involved in some of these initiatives and I have visited/researched others. In this text, however, I do not seek to analyze or represent the intentions of the organizers/collectives that initiated them, but rather I attempt to theorize—through these momentums—potential instituent counterstrategies of (un)making spaces of culture.

4   Stefano Harney and Fred Moten, *The Undercommons: Fugitive Planning & Black Study*. New York: Minor Compositions, 2013, p. 64.

Teatro Valle Occupato, the banner hanging from the balcony reads: "COME TRISTE LA PRUDENZA!" (How sad is prudence). Photo: CC Teatro Valle Occupato

Teatro Valle, situated in Rome's historical center, was the city's oldest functioning theater. In 2010, after a change in Italian cultural policy that was gearing towards privatization, Teatro Valle was closed by the Minister of Economy and Finance on the grounds of its assumed "lack of utility." The strategy of the Italian government to generate revenue by private investment resulted in a series of institutions failing "to remain financially viable and [having] to close, including Teatro Valle."[5] On June 14, 2011, the day after a national referendum in which the Italian people overwhelmingly voted to reclaim water as a common resource, the abandoned Teatro Valle was occupied by a diverse group of people working in the arts and culture. As stated by the occupiers:

5   Alice Borchi, "Teatro Valle Occupato: Protesting, Occupying and Making Art in Contemporary Italy," *Research in Drama Education: The Journal of Applied Theatre and Performance*, vol. 22, no. 1, (2017), pp. 126–29, here p. 127.

The Teatro Valle is not only a valuable space to be saved but a
symbol of the state of Art in Italy. We are here to become pro-
tagonists in the political decisions that affect our industry, our
work, our lives. We are here to imagine and build together the
theater that we would like. Lacking any form of dialogue and
having witnessed every principle of representation ignored, we
want to reclaim the places that belong to us. We want to participate in the political processes that decide the fate of our lives
and the culture of our country.[6]

Built in 1726 by architect Tommaso Morelli, Teatro Valle hosted numerous operas and dramas during the eighteenth century and was
also the first Italian theater to welcome the general public, rather than
exclusively the aristocracy.[7] In this structure, designed for a culture
of past times, a new public space was created that offered a function-
al operational model and a different collective cultural imaginary in
the here and now. During the years of the occupation, Teatro Valle
hosted multiple events and became a space for social, political, and
cultural practices based around ideas of the "common good."

What are the emergent and dependent relations amidst the built
form, the spatial structure, the operational model, and the surroundings? How can these ongoing and repeated spatial and timely dialogues co-produce a space and form its imaginary? Marianne Van
Kerkhoven writes, "around the production lies the theatre and around
the theatre lies the city and around the city, as far as we can see, lies the
whole world and even the sky and all its stars. The walls that link all
these circles together are made of skin, they have pores, they breathe."[8]
How are the spaces formed in which figurative publics take place? In

6   Teatro Valle Occupato, "The Occupation of Teatro Valle, Rome" (July 29,
    2011), http://www.teatrovalleoccupato.it/the-occupation-of-teatro-valle-
    rome, accessed September 20, 2022.
7   Saki Bailey and Maria Edgarda Marcucci, "Legalizing the Occupation:
    The Teatro Valle as a Cultural Commons," *South Atlantic Quarterly*,
    vol. 112, no. 2 (2013), pp. 396–405, here p. 397.
8   Marianne Van Kerkhoven, "The theatre is in the city and the city is in the
    world and its walls are of skin," *Etcetera* (October 1994), http://sarma.be/
    docs/3229, accessed November 22, 2022.

what ways do the surrounding rhythms, breaths, and movements affect their structure? How might they be dependent upon the surrounding environment and yet open up space for what could be otherwise?

Material relations and dependencies form the way we make and
inhabit spaces. To recognize material dependencies in processes of
instituting means to work with and against horizons of expectation
and existing imaginaries. Teatro Valle Occupato offers an example of
an operational model, a dislocated DIY institution, that negotiates
these material micro/macro relations through a specific building. In
a space that was built for the large-scale shows of times past, this collective mobilization offered new ways to reinhabit its abandoned
structure in the center of the city. Teatro Valle Occupato offered a par-
adigm of how an occupation might make an intervention in both the
city and in the field of law by putting forward a proposition for a new
legal form: the institution of the commons. In collaboration with law-
yers/jurists Ugo Mattei and Stefano Rodotà, Teatro Valle Occupato
created the Fondazione Teatro Valle Bene Comune (Teatro Valle Common Good Foundation). The proposition put forward by Fondazione
Teatro Valle Bene Comune sought to maintain the ethos of open participation and yet propose a specific legal entity that supports processes
of commoning. According to Mattei, bottom-up structures that demand
visibility and then legitimacy might hold the potential to penetrate the
neoliberal order and produce new forms inside the system.[9] In other
words, such legal modalities might create and legitimize a framework
that institutes a different social ecology and set of relations that promote and support collective structures. Even if Mattei's proposition is
debatable as to how much one can do with the "tools of the master,"
this example of collective intervention in the space of the city and, at
the same time, in the space of the law offers interesting pathways to
rethink issues of continuity, collectivity, and instituting.

The Teatro Valle occupation ended in August 2014 after the occupiers gave up the space to the city of Rome in order for them to proceed with plans for restoration with the promise that the occupiers

9   Ugo Mattei, "The New Institutions of The Commons," paper presented
    at SpielArt *Wake Up!* Festival, Munich, November 25–27, 2013.

would be involved again in the management of the space at a later stage. Several years later, the space remains closed, and the issue continues to be controversial among participants and audiences. Despite its abrupt ending, Teatro Valle Occupato offered no less than an important legacy.

Material dependencies are inscribed in both the physical and immaterial environment. As Doreen Massey argues, "architecture" is never limited to what is there; she states that, "the spaces of social relations are constructed, just as buildings are constructed; they can be adapted, as buildings can be adapted; they are not 'material' as buildings are material, but they can be as hard to walk through as a wall."[10] Recognizing material dependencies and immaterial walls opens up ways to connect with what happened, but also with what might happen in the here and now. Places are the product of material embodied practices, which even after their physical disappearance continue to affect through invisible material traces, inscribed in the streets and seats, in galleries and amphitheaters, in quiet corners and restrooms. The spaces around us host genealogies of practice and histories of struggle, nonlinear constellations of space and time that might offer ways to practice anew material and immaterial reconfigurations of space, (de)instituent forms that propose strategies to inhabit otherwise the here and now.

2. Unsettling

How can we more intensely feel the physics of our surround, our social aesthetic, the gravity of our love and loss, our shared, radically sounded, radically sent incompleteness?[11]

10 Doreen Massey, "Living in Wythenshawe," in Alicia Pivaro et al. (eds), *The Unknown City: Contesting Architecture and Social Space*. Cambridge, MA: MIT Press, 2002, pp. 458–75, here p. 472.
11 Stefano Harney and Fred Moten, *All Incomplete*. Colchester, CT: Minor Compositions, 2021, p. 26.

> Every social stratum has its own 'Common Sense' and its own 'Good Sense,' which are basically the most widespread conception of life and of man.[12]

How do we unsettle, decompose in order to compose again, and blur relations between the "instituted and the institutions" of the society, "common sense" and its expected horizons of expectation? To unsettle is to shake the webs of legibility that form worldviews and the repetitive attitudes that compose the "ways things are." Unsettling as the interconnected practice of making through experimenting or experimenting through making, what Harney and Moten refer to when they write "our real purpose of 'making' is to encourage possibilities for presencing in and through experimentation."[13] How might this making through experimentation or experimenting through making offer forms of presencing as we compose, discompose, and recompose contexts, spaces, and practices?

Revisiting the example of the Embros theater activation in November 2011, I would propose "unsettling" as a curatorial method of intervening in existing narratives when (un)making sites of culture. Recognizing material dependencies, histories, and modus operandi seems an essential step, but how might we then start experimenting with such relations and dependencies in order to allow other spaces, contexts, and publics to emerge—to evolve contexts and shared spaces that belong to no one and resist categorization and structuralization?

Embros was a disused theater in the center of Athens. A print house in the 1930s and a popular theater and drama school in the 1990s, it played a significant role in the cultural production of the city. After the death of the theater director who was running the space in 2007, the state-owned theater remained closed. The Mavili Collective,[14] a spontaneously assembled group of performance makers and

---

12 Antonio Gramsci, *Selections from Prison Notebooks*, ed. and trans. Quintin Hoare and Geoffrey Nowell Smith. New York: International Publishers, 1971, p. 326.

13 Harney and Moten, *All Incomplete*, p. 271.

14 The Mavili Collective came together in 2010 and, prior to the occupation of the Embros theater, had created a series of collective contexts that questioned cultural policies.

theorists, occupied the theater in November 2011 as a symbolic act
that sought to activate city spaces and offer unexpected cultural
forms. On the morning of the official opening, a press conference was
organized in the building where audiences, inhabitants, cultural
workers, journalists, and anarchists coexisted, and a manifesto was
sent out to the press:

> Today 11 November 2011 Mavili Collective occupied the histor-
> ical disused theatre building of Embros in Athens, deserted
> and left empty for years by the Greek Ministry of Culture. [...]
> For the next 11 days Mavili will reconstitute Embros as a public
> space for exchange, research, debate, meeting and re-thinking.
> [...] This model emerges from the current lacks and shortfalls
> of our system and attempts to interrogate the global changing
> landscape at this moment in time. We challenge our own limits
> and understanding and we propose to operate this space as a
> constantly re-evaluated model by both ourselves and the pub-
> lic—an open system that might offer the potential to re-think
> relations between people and possible roles for art in society.
> [...] We actively propose new structures, which we hope, can
> become sites of negotiation, debate, re-formulation.[15]

Instead of symbolically occupying the space, this action proposed a
form of intervention by initiating an intense twelve-day public program that sought to actively intervene in the modus operandi of the
sociocultural Greek landscape. By unsetting expectations, the hybrid
program—instead of a curatorial statement or theme—proposed
modes of intervention that the 291 participants were called to inhabit,
experiment in, and create work for. Although the intervention took
place inside a traditional theater setting, the program refused to host
modes of drama, dance, and music that were already made/complete
and proposed instead hybrid forms, incomplete experimentations and

---

15 Mavili Collective, A Temporary Re-Activation of Disused Building,
    "Mavili Collective: re-activate manifesto" (November 11, 2011),
    http://mavilicollective.wordpress.com/re-activate/, accessed
    August 19, 2020.

collaborations. Hosting work by recognized artists and professors, as well as by students and marginalized communities, the program resisted categorization and was reprinted/reformed daily to allow more participation in response to the initial strands of the program.

This attempt both to recognize and unsettle material relations was also associated with Mavili's commitment to experimental practice. Resisting the creation of an alternative space that would reproduce the dominant aesthetics of representation, this occupation sought to bring experimental practice in form and in context for the purposes of exploring practices that might intervene in social and political realities. Through this practice of unsettling, the program reflected upon existing narratives and aesthetics that formed the cultural imaginary while experimenting with forms of doing otherwise. Through unsettling and experimenting, the Embros occupation attempted to critically intervene in the here and now of the Greek cultural landscape and rehearse other modes of instituting, perhaps as a dislocated institution in a social space.

The Embros occupation, 2011. The artwork on the wall is by Alexandros Mistriotis in response to the "one-day residency" program, it reads:
"Σου γραφω γιατι ξερω οτι θα ξεχαστουν αυτες οι μερες"
(I am writing to you 'cause I know these days will be forgotten).
Photo: Georgios Makkas

Harney and Moten write that the blurred form suggests "something in excess, a refusal to be straightened, a syncopation in the rhythm that kills, a collapse of our ordering in spacetime, of the linearity of space and time itself."[16] Through unsettling existing relations and horizons of expectations and comprehensibility, as Embros did, an unexpected space might be created, a blurred form that appears unidentifiable and illegible, a shared space that belongs to no one. Experimenting and thus unsettling—or unsettling and thus experimenting—as a questioning of personal and collective methods and sedimented practices might also create blurred interplays between different social forms and categorizations. Harney and Moten ask further: "what if, through our entangled, incomplete sociality, we could engender this blur of/as 'always forming but never completing' to dissolve the imposition of photographic subjectivities particularized into the distinct perspectives of the maker, sitter, viewer, seller, buyer, teacher, critic?"[17]

These multiple layers of unsettling in form, content, relations, and modes of production have the potential to give rise to the emergence of a blurred and shared form that opens up other narratives of practice and action. A blurred form that refuses categorization and distinct perspectives and thus holds the potential to produce a shared space "always forming but never completing"; an ephemeral site of an otherwise, a "concrete elsewhere." Such blurred places of figurative publics offer reconfigurations of space and time and reorganizations of the commons of social production through new paradigms of institutional forms that remain responsive—through interplays of experimenting, making, and tearing apart again and again. Vulnerable and broken forms of practice that embrace both instituting and de-instituting and question both positionally, and question the potential of movement, the necessity of being moved, located, and dislocated, starting again "with the same joke, the same story, always elsewhere."[18]

After a year and repeated attempts by the state and the police to privatize it and close it down, Embros changed its mode of operation and began to resample the operational model of other squats and oc-

---

16 Harney and Moten, *All Incomplete*, p. 56.
17 Ibid., p. 171.
18 Harney and Moten, *The Undercommons*, p. 64.

cupied spaces in the city; in this way, it continues until today as a po-
litical/cultural space. At the same time, the curatorial approach of the
public program that combined different forms and hybrid collective
practices, theoretical production, artistic practice, and social/politi-
cal praxis, formed a method that was replicated numerous times by
other institutions both DIY and dominant in the Greek cultural landscape. Yet this practice of unsettling, of blurring rather than reproduc-
ing and fixing the form, was lost somewhere in this reproduction;
with it, the unidentified potential that haunted these days of November 2011 was also lost.

3. Incomprehensibility

What is a public institution? What is, for example, a city hall?
Is this magical place, this mythical place, this imaginary place
where, so they have told us, our sovereignty resides, nothing
more or less than our political will? What is an institution? Is it
that pretty legend of the people freely ceding its representation?
Ceding it to who? What is a town hall? Is it perhaps a place of
fantasy in which, so they tell us time and again, we have given
to a few the privilege of speaking in our name? Does this place
really exist? Has anyone ever seen it?[19]

La Casa Invisible is situated in the touristic part of Malaga city center,
a nineteenth-century building that was occupied in 2007 and func-
tions as a cultural-social space resistant to the touristification of the
city. Entering the closed shared yard in front of the building of La
Casa Invisible feels like taking a wrong turn and ending up somewhere
else, an elsewhere, outside this city and its commercialized business-
es. The temporary configurations of tables and chairs and the informal
gatherings taking place create another spatial grammar to the repeated configurations of bars and restaurants in the streets of Malaga. España and Raunig discuss the city of unattractive attractions and argue

---

19 Casa Invisible, "Manifiesto 27 November 2021," trans. Kelly Mulvaney,
    transversal texts, https://transversal.at/blog/manifiesto-27-november-2021,
    accessed March 11, 2022.

that it "has always been the showcase of experiments with governmental forms [...] the city is where life escapes," while at the same
time they also argue that one can find in the city "subsistential territories [...] in which things, machines, animals, and people actually
ek-sist alongside one another and live together."[20] Inside La Casa Invisible and this territory/building, one can see the multiple layers of
cultural activities that have taken place there, that seem out of sync
with the surrounding area and its dominant forms. Writing for La
Casa Invisible, Raunig has said:

> Casa Invisible has been a guarantor of alternative cultures and
> ecologies of care, and it has also been a social machine for ev-
> erything that is incompliant in spite of, and in the middle of,
> the compliant city: feminist cafes and workshops, antiracist
> and refugees-welcome groups, concerts, local meetings of the
> PAH (platform against evictions), meetings of the movement
> Málaga no se vende and of the Sindicato Inquilinas, discursive
> events held by the Universidad Libre Experimental (ULEX),
> dance and theatre workshops, technopolitical initiatives, and
> much more.[21]

Searching for La Casa Invisible in English online, one can only find
some reviews from Trip Advisor that describe it as "a secret place in
the middle," "a pleasant bar," "a lovely alternative spot." What most
descriptions share is a confusion as to what this space is really for and
how it operates; it seems unintelligible within the existing urban
grammar of the city. Someone writes "we found this wonderful place
by chance and returned for several nights but was unclear what it is,"
while someone else comments "we never got to the bottom of how it
came to be in existence but there is a story there!" Denise Ferreira da

20 Kike España and Gerald Raunig, "The City of Attractions," *transversal
    texts* (April 2019), https://transversal.at/blog/The-City-of-Attractions,
    accessed March 11, 2022.
21 Gerald Raunig, "La Casa Invisible is here to stay: Against the eviction of
    the Invisible, against Mall-aga, against the compliant city," trans. Kelly
    Mulvaney, *transversal texts* (July 2018), https://transversal.at/blog/
    Invisible-is-here-to-stay, accessed March 11, 2022.

erasure

debtors

Silva refers to "incomprehensibility" in relation to incompleteness in the introduction to Harney and Moten's book *All Incomplete*, writing "Incomprehension [...] recalls how formality and efficacy both request and give completeness. That which does not exhibit either cannot be seen as total, finalized, absolute, or perfect. It is not then comprehensible: it does not explain (account for) itself, either all of its various parts or as a whole."[22] The Invisible Committee argue that "if the institution suits us so well, it's because the sort of legibility it guarantees saves us above all, each one of us [...] from producing together an intelligibility of the world that is properly ours and shared in common."[23] How, then, might practices that refuse to be complete, formal, closed, and legible create incomprehensible instituent territories that contest the dominant governmental forms? How might this practice of being out of sync/dislocating/contesting what is dominant and legible offer ways to practice the "intelligibility of the world that is properly ours and shared in common"? How, then, does this noncompliant incomprehensibility create the conditions for other narratives and ways of (un)making sense?

La Casa Invisible. The banner hanging on the back wall reads, "derecho a la ciudad" (right to the city). 2017. Photo: Kike España

22 Denise Ferreira da Silva, "Foreword," in Moten and Harney, *All Incomplete*, pp. 5–11, here p. 6.
23 The Invisible Committee, *Now*, p. 70.

La Casa Invisible and the other examples discussed in previous sec-
tions are not spaces of alterity—on the contrary, they are spaces deeply rooted and engaged in the city, its surrounding environment, its
struggles, its dominant modes of production. Resisting the formality of
a complete structure through their dislocated positionality, they make
space for what has not yet been accepted or absorbed by the dominant
form, allowing other ways of being to materialize. Incomprehensibility appears as a possible strategy in making such spaces that contest
urban narratives and make possible other reconfigurations. Such sites
that engage with material dependencies, unsettle existing cultural
imaginaries, and make space for the incomprehensible and the incomplete hold the potential to give visibility to an otherwise. This otherwise often appears incomprehensible, as it questions the legibility
of the pre-given structures. Yet this practice of experimenting with
forms of being and doing together, dislocating existing narratives,
might offer ephemeral presencings of other unfamiliar worldviews.

4. Brokenness/Vulnerability

Lauren Berlant, in discussing possible structures for transitional
times, proposed the term "transformational infrastructures" to describe the practice of generating "a form from within brokenness beyond the exigencies of the current crisis, and alternatively to it too."[24]
As Berlant argues, infrastructures are not the same thing as institutions, since "infrastructures are there for use," further proposing an
ability "to be in the space of broken form and nonetheless understand
that as you proceed transformation can proceed."[25]

Several years after the economic crisis of June 2015 in Athens at
a moment of hopeful brokenness, following years of organizing and
ephemerally making and tearing apart bottom-up solidarity structures, an "unidentified" collective that consisted of members of the
Embros theater occupation and other cultural workers initiated a new

24 Lauren Berlant, "The Commons: Infrastructures for Troubling Times,"
    Environment and Planning D: Society and Space, vol. 34, no. 3 (2016),
    pp. 393–419, here p. 393.
25 Lauren Berlant, "Q&A about transformational infrastructures,"
    presented at the public program *In Spite of Everything: Stubborn Returns
    and Urban Afterlives*, Athens, May 25, 2017.

cultural occupancy in a disused building (Green Park café) in Pedion tou Areos, one of the two central parks of Athens. As stated in the manifesto:

> Almost 4 years after the occupation of the Embros theatre in 2011 we are activating with our own means a space deserted and left empty for years by the Greek state and propose a 10-day program of cultural and political intervention in the here and now of Athens [...]. We propose friendship as a model for organizational formations and autonomous instituting that exceeds neo-liberal calls to order. Deploying friendship [...] in a struggle against cultural and artistic monopolies, 'creative cities' and their production lines of co-optation, through this ephemeral collective experiment we aim to co-imagine with fellow city dwellers, the here and now of Green Park and our city.[26]

The space experimented with different forms of participation that tested how a cultural space might operate in these times of crises and impoverishment. The door was always half-open, and artistic, academic, and other social activities were accessible to anyone, transparent to the city, contesting the production of meaning. Operating solely via social media, Green Park drew large audiences with an irregular pattern of activities, varying in density and frequency, resisting the performance of an identity. As Berlant argues, infrastructures are not the same thing as institutions, and, as such, this collective vulnerable infrastructure, in seeking to explore forms of politics and joy, was defined by its use, testing processes of instituting in the here and now. During these years, Green Park hosted conferences, talks, residencies, artistic projects, neighborhood meetings, a DIY performance biennial, concerts, and solidarity events that reinformed each other, constantly affected by the urgent needs of the project's surroundings. Located in the heart of the city and amidst its crisis, away from the gentrified parts of Athens, artistic and political activities took place where diverse audiences mixed, producing an unexpected, and at times even uncomfortable, public space that questioned methods of cultural/theoretical/political production.

26 Green Park Athens, "Manifesto" (2015), https://greenparkathens. wordpress.com/manifesto/, accessed August 19, 2017.

Green Park, "Where Are We Now: Struggling Autonomies in Closing Times," an exhibition and a series of discussions. The photograph depicts one of the discussions with Jacques Rancière together with Stavros Stavridis, Akis Gavrilidis, Evangelia Ledaki, Kostis Velonis, and Despina Zefkili. On the back wall, the letters form the question "Where are we Now?," June 2017. Photo: G. Argyropoulou

In her discussion about institutionalization and precarity Bojana Kunst argues that the question of the institution should be linked to changes in precarity in order to understand the paradoxical dynamic of their political and social position. Kunst refers to a talk by Athena Athanasiou that took place in Green Park as part of the conference "Institutions, Politics, Performance":

> Her lecture was held in an old abandoned theatre, which was taken over by a collective and transferred into the temporal venue, a conference meeting, but also a temporal retreat at the same time for refugees [...]. So, in Green Park, Athena Athanasiou talked about the paradoxical conditionality of the institutions [...].

[A] conditionality, which enables the simultaneity between performing the institution and resisting the very process of institutionalisation.[27]

Kunst proposes that experimental processes of institutionalization should be poetic, that is, they should lead to a specific production of forms that behave more "like a plant, a weed, stuck in the ground but nevertheless connected with the surrounding habitat, an earthly infrastructure."[28] Green Park continued for two years, resistant to processes of institutionalization and yet confronting the vital need for forms and infrastructures that support life and provide glimpses of an elsewhere—spatially, socially, and culturally. The fluidity of the structure resisted translation into a stable modus operandi, and the space way-found vulnerability through personal relations. Green Park continued as a process through unstable formations and without support in exceedingly vulnerable surroundings. It reflected perhaps one temporal position in between brokenness and making, performing the institution and resisting institutionalization, between dislocating and relocating, in a decomposed and recomposed movement, in between dominant powers, vulnerable bodies, and buildings.

Dislocating Institutions, Practicing Out Of Sync

Pablo Carmona and co-authors discuss social centers as a kind of public square for emergent subjectivities and bearers of a new kind of institutionality.[29] They discuss the possibility of "effective movement institutions" where more efficacious forms of politics can be practiced,

27 Bojana Kunst, "The Institutionalisation, Precarity and the Rhythm of Work," Flanders Arts Institute (May 4, 2020), https://www.kunsten.be/en/now-in-the-arts/the-institutionalisation-precarity-and-the-rhythm-of-work/, accessed March 11, 2022.

28 Ibid.

29 Pablo Carmona, Tomás Herreros, Raúl Sánchez Cedillo, and Nicolás Sguiglia, "Social Centres: Monsters and Political Machines for a New Generation of Movement Institutions," *transversal texts* (April 2008), https://transversal.at/transversal/0508/sguiglia-sanchez-cedillo-carmona-herreros/en?hl=casa%2520invisible, accessed March 11, 2022.

arguing that "we miss the presence of more institutions of this kind: institutions that are flexible, mobile, nomadic and inserted in the swarm of the multitude. Institutions that arise from the sedimentation of previous mobilisations."[30]

Momentums like the ones discussed in this text offer transformative instituent counterstrategies that rethink cultural imaginaries within specific milieus. Perhaps as "effective movement institutions" or DIY dislocated cultural institutions, these momentums embodied the sedimentation of previous movements and at the same time became places for new forms of social improvisation. Thus, these momentums of (un)making spaces of culture manifested and gave rise to institutional forms that operate as social processes. These practices emerged, in a sense, from the contradiction that Athanasiou considers critical for the institution today and includes both "the necessity to sustain human beings and the violence that can destroy human beings."[31] Material dependencies, unsettling, incomprehensibility, and brokenness have been proposed as potential key strategies in dislocating the institution as we know it and, thus, making future sites that allow reconfigurations of an otherwise to ephemerally take form. Being out of sync/contesting what is dominant and legible, such practices offer instances of being and doing together that at times reveal an "intelligibility of the world that is properly ours and shared in common."[32]

Employing dislocating as a practice of necessity and as a possible strategy that blurs the familiar can offer structures that remain illegible to processes of locating, structurization, and recuperation. Dislocating, thus, becomes this practice of presencing an otherwise that currently cannot be fully realized within existing strictures, a rehearsing of an "earthly" transformational infrastructure. Multiplying such practices of dislocating can perhaps bring into being other social ecologies, histories, and constellations that can continuously give rise to ephemeral incomprehensible "subsistential territories" and figurative publics that embody the vulnerability of making—an instituent practice that acknowledges the vulnerability of bodies and the surrounding

---

30 Ibid.
31 Quoted from Kunst, "The Institutionalisation, Precarity and the Rhythm of Work."
32 The Invisible Committee, *Now*, p. 70.

habitat and, thus, embraces discontinuity, brokenness, unsettledness, dependency, and other human and more-than-human qualities. Pre-sensing, sketching, and practicing together supportive infrastructures and other forms of life. Emergent. Fleeing. Always elsewhere. Always present, here and now.

Special thanks to Pantxo Ramas, Alice Borchi, Gerald Raunig, and Kike España for directing me to research the material that have helped to form this work; Stefanie Sachsenmaier for useful comments; and of course, to Bernd Scherer for his invitation to contribute this text, and many formative discussions.

+   **Bernd Scherer, Director of Haus der Kulturen der Welt (HKW) from 2006 to 2022, took up the role having previously been Director of the Goethe-Institut in Mexico. A philosopher and author of numerous publications, his theoretical focus is on aesthetics, philosophy of language, semiotics, and international cultural exchange. He has curated and co-curated several cultural and art projects including *Agua-Wasser* (2003), *Über Lebenskunst* (2010–11), *The Anthropocene Project* (2013–14), *100 Years of Now* (2015–19), and *The New Alphabet* (2019–22). Since January 2011, he has also been teaching at the Institute for European Ethnology, Humboldt-Universität zu Berlin. Among the many publications he has edited or co-edited are *Das Anthropozän. Zum Stand der Dinge* (2015), the four-volume work *Textures of the Anthropocene: Grain Vapor Ray* (2015), *Die Zeit der Algorithmen* (2016), and *Wörterbuch der Gegenwart* (2019). In 2022 he published *Der Angriff der Zeichen. Denkbilder und Handlungsmuster des Anthropozäns.***

+   Gigi Argyropoulou is a theorist, curator, dramaturge, and practitioner working in the fields of performance and cultural practice. She received her PhD from the University of Roehampton London and has organized public programs, interventions, performances, exhibitions, and festivals both inside and outside of institutions, she also publishes regularly in books and journals. She co-initiated the first DIY Performance Biennial "No Future" in 2016 and Οχτώ/Eight (Critical institute for arts and politics) in Athens. She was co-editor of the 2015 special issue of *Performance Research* "On Institutions."

+   Maria Hlavajova is an organizer, researcher, educator, curator, and founding general and artistic director of BAK, basis voor actuele kunst, Utrecht (since 2000). Between 2008 and 2016, she was research and artistic director of the collaborative research, exhibition, and education project FORMER WEST, which culminated in the publication *Former West: Art and the Contemporary After 1989* (co-edited with Simon Sheikh, 2016). She is a lecturer at HKU University of the Arts Utrecht and the Academy of Fine Arts and Design, Bratislava. In the recent past, Hlavajova served on the supervisory boards of the Amsterdam-based European Cultural Foundation and Stedelijk Museum.

+   Olaf Nicolai's work has been shown in numerous international solo exhibitions, most recently at Kunstsammlungen Chemnitz (2020), Museum of Monash University (MUMA), Melbourne (2019), Kunsthalle Wien (2018), and the German Pavilion at the 56th Biennale di Venezia (2015). His awards include the Art Prize of the City of Wolfsburg (2002) and the Karl Sczuka Prize for Radio Art (2017) for his contribution *In the woods there is a bird...* to documenta 14. He teaches at the Academy of Fine Arts Munich.

+   Adania Shibli was born in Palestine and has written novels, plays, short stories, and narrative essays. Shibli has twice been awarded with the Qattan Young Writer's Award-Palestine: in 2001 for her novel *Masaas* and in 2003 for her novel *Kulluna Ba'id bethat al Miqdar aan el-Hub.* Her latest novel, *Tafsil Thanawi* (2017)—translated into English as *Minor Detail* (2020)— was nominated for the National Book Award 2020 and the International Booker Prize 2021. Shibli is also engaged in academic research and teaching.

+   Eyal Weizman is founding Director of the multidisciplinary research group Forensic Architecture and Professor of Spatial and Visual Cultures at Goldsmiths, University of London. He is the author of over fifteen books, including *Hollow Land* (2007), *The Roundtable Revolution* (2015), and *Investigative Aesthetics* (2021). He is also a member of the Technology Advisory Board of the International Criminal Court and the Centre for Investigative Journalism.

Das Neue Alphabet (The New Alphabet) is a publication series by HKW (Haus der Kulturen der Welt).

The series is part of the HKW project *Das Neue Alphabet* (2019–2022), supported by the Federal Government Commissioner for Culture and the Media due to a ruling of the German Bundestag.

Series Editors: Detlef Diederichsen, Anselm Franke,
      Katrin Klingan, Daniel Neugebauer, Bernd Scherer
Project Management: Philipp Albers
Managing Editor: Martin Hager
Copy-Editing: Mandi Gomez, Hannah Sarid de Mowbray
Design Concept: Olaf Nicolai with Malin Gewinner,
      Hannes Drißner

Vol. 25: *The New Institution*
Editor: Bernd Scherer
Coordination: Philipp Albers
Contributors: Gigi Argyropoulou, Maria Hlavajova, Olaf Nicolai,
      Adania Shibli, Eyal Weizman
Translation: Faith Ann Gibson
Graphic Design: Malin Gewinner, Hannes Drißner,
      Markus Dreßen, Lyosha Kritsouk
DNA-Lettering (Cover): Nelly Nakahara
Type-Setting: Lyosha Kritsouk
Fonts: FK Raster (Florian Karsten), Suisse BP Int'l (Ian Party)
      Lyon Text (Kai Bernau)
Image Editing: ScanColor Reprostudio GmbH, Leipzig
Printing and Binding: Gutenberg Beuys Feindruckerei GmbH,
      Langenhagen

pp. 6/7, 16/17, 34/35, 48/49, 66/67, 82/83 Olaf Nicolai, *Up, Down and Around* (6 Inserts), watercolor on hand-made paper and digital drawing (10,5 × 15 cm), 2022. Courtesy: Olaf Nicolai and Galerie EIGEN+ART Leipzig / Berlin. Scans and image editing of watercolors: Jan Scheffler (Prints Professional)

Published by:
Spector Books
Harkortstr. 10
01407 Leipzig
www.spectorbooks.com

Distribution:
Germany, Austria: GVA Gemeinsame Verlagsauslieferung
Göttingen GmbH & Co. KG, www.gva-verlage.de
Switzerland: AVA Verlagsauslieferung AG, www.ava.ch
France, Belgium: Interart Paris, www.interart.fr
UK: Central Books Ltd, www.centralbooks.com
USA, Canada, Central and South America, Africa:
ARTBOOK | D.A.P. www.artbook.com
Japan: twelvebooks, www.twelve-books.com
South Korea: The Book Society, www.thebooksociety.org
Australia, New Zealand: Perimeter Distribution,
www.perimeterdistribution.com

Haus der Kulturen der Welt
John-Foster-Dulles-Allee 10
D-10557 Berlin
www.hkw.de

Haus der Kulturen der Welt

Haus der Kulturen der Welt is a business division of Kultur-
veranstaltungen des Bundes in Berlin GmbH (KBB).

Director: Bernd Scherer
Managing Director: Charlotte Sieben
Chairwoman of the Supervisory Board: Claudia Roth MdB
Federal Government Commissioner for Culture and the Media

Haus der Kulturen der Welt is supported by

 Minister of State for Culture and the Media   NEU START KULTUR  Federal Foreign Office

First Edition
Printed in Germany
ISBN: 978-3-95905-666-3